Will Smith

The Freshest Prince

Will Smith
The Freshest Prince

BY MARK BEGO

A JOHN BOSWELL ASSOCIATES BOOK

Andrews McMeel
Publishing

Kansas City

www.andrewsmcmeel.com

Library of Congress Cataloging-in-Publication Data on file
ISBN: 0-8362-7132-7

Cover and book design by
Charles Kreloff

DEDICATION

To the one and only Martha Reeves. Thank you for inspiring the whole world to go "Dancing in the Street" with you, and special thanks for being such a wonderful friend to me. More fun to come . . . I promise! —Mark Bego

ACKNOWLEDGMENTS

Robert Bennett
Eden Blackwood
John Boswell and Patty Brown
Trippy Cunningham
William Dawson
Glenn Hughes
Isiah James
Christine Jampolsky
Charles Kreloff
Sindi Markoff Kaplan
Marsha Rosco
Ruffa & Ruffa
Peter Schekeryk and Melanie
Jim Thompson and Melitta Coffee
Stanley Turer
Mary Wilson

Contents

Gettin' Jiggy Wit It

He's handsome, he's multitalented, and he has a steadfast and sincere list of moralistic convictions. As a teenager he established himself as one of the most successful rap vocalists of the late 1980s. Then he conquered the competitive world of network television. Now, in the past five years, he has established himself as one of the hottest film stars of the 1990s. He is so successful, in fact, that three of his most recent movies have grossed over $100 million each at the

Will Smith is currently on a hot streak, on the record charts and in the movies.

Oprah Winfrey, Will Smith, and Jada Pinkett at the Academy Awards presentation, 1996.

most successful television series—black or white—of the 1990s. His movies, including *Independence Day*, *Made in America*, and *Men in Black*, have made him a modern-day box-office legend. And his recent movie star marriage to the beautiful and talented Jada Pinkett has made his personal existence a Hollywood fairy tale. In a world of stereotypes, Will has created a career by clearing his own distinctly unique path through the often treacherous show business wilderness.

His show business career started in his hometown of Philadelphia, Pennsylvania, more than ten years ago. Joining forces with a local buddy, Jeff Townes, Smith became the "fresh" half of the rap recording duo D.J. Jazzy Jeff & the Fresh Prince. Almost instantly they experienced a huge avalanche of media coverage, record sales, television appearances, and all of the trappings associated with fame.

Right after Jazzy Jeff & the Fresh Prince's first brushes with success Will went wild with out-of-control spending. He had sold millions of recordings, and money seemed to flow in at a seemingly never-ending rate. Still a teenager at the time, he never took into account that the Internal Revenue

box-office. His rap records are known for their up-beat, clean, and positive messages. And in the movies he is known for his infectiously genuine smile and winning personality. Yet, for Will Smith, it's all just another honest day's work.

His recordings of "Parents Just Don't Understand," "Summertime," and "Men in Black" have all won him Grammy awards. His television show, *The Fresh Prince of Bel Air*, has the distinction of being one of the

Service would eventually be expecting a tax payment from him. He went from rich at 18 years old, to nearly bankrupt at 19.

Thankfully, through a chance meeting in Los Angeles in 1990, Will Smith found himself the star of his own network television show. With a touch of maturity, and the granted wish of a second chance, this time around he handled money and fame in a much more mature and methodical fashion. The reward has been the career peaks he is now experiencing.

With the positive, articulate, well-groomed image that Will Smith projects—currently and in the past—few can fault him for the path he has chosen. Whenever a challenge has come his way, time and time again he has elected to pursue his goals in his own distinctive way, and his choices have almost always spelled success.

In a competitive music business atmosphere where some people consider "pop" records white music and rap records are considered black music, Will Smith has bridged the gap between the two audiences. To prove that Will Smith is at the top of his game, in 1997 he turned the song "Men in Black" into the most listened-to rap song in the history of the entire genre. However, he is not without

Will Smith, Patti LaBelle, Luther Vandross, and Vanessa Williams at the Soul Train Awards.

his detractors. His black rap rivals have been especially stinging in their criticism of his recordings, his television show, and his career choices. Most of these claims can be directly written off to sheer jealousy.

After *The Fresh Prince of Bel Air* became a top-rated television show, Will found himself longing to break into feature films. He cut his teeth in front of the movie cameras on a low-budget but notable film called *Where the Day*

Takes You in 1992. The next year he followed it up with the highly prestigious *Six Degrees of Separation*. After those performances came the Whoopi Goldberg comedy *Made in America* and a cop film called *Bad Boys*.

In 1996, right after *The Fresh Prince of Bel Air* finished its last season, Will was seen on the big screen in the exciting science fiction action film *Independence Day*. When that film was released July fourth weekend and became

No longer content to follow the pack, Smith proudly marches to the beat of a different drummer.

the most popular film of the entire year, Smith's stature in Hollywood suddenly went through the roof.

Although network television was unhappy to see him disappear from their roster, nearly everyone who ever met him is happy for his newfound mega-success as a full-fledged movie star. Says Warren Littlefield, NBC-TV Entertainment president, "Will Smith is a rocket ship. He took off and just kept going."

While *The Fresh Prince of Bel Air* placed him in people's living rooms once a week, a career in films has taken his fame, and magnified it enormously. According to him, "I was recognized from TV, but this is way beyond that. With TV, I guess people feel like they invite you into their homes. The day before *Independence Day* opened, people on the street were like, 'Will, what's up?' The day after, it was, 'Hey, Mr. Smith. How are you?' There's a whole different level of respect."

The following July he was back on the screen in the tongue-in-cheek intergalactic smash *Men in Black*. The next thing he knew, he was an even bigger international success than he ever dreamed of becoming.

With his own warm sense of humor he simply stated, "It's just my job to save the world every summer. I really don't know what I'm going to do for an encore next year. But it has to be something big on the July fourth weekend."

Although his next film missed the Independence Day schedule, his new 1998 film, *Enemy of the State*, has made a worthy follow-up to the winning streak that *Independence Day* and *Men in Black* created the two previous

Will with Little Richard and M.C. Hammer on the set of *The Arsenio Hall Show*.

summers. After two consecutive years of contending with creatures from other planets, Smith is the first to admit that he is happily taking a break from fighting alien invaders. "I've done so many alien movies," he quips, "that I'm going to team with Sigourney Weaver to do the next *Alien*. Except the poster will read 'Will Smith *IS* the Alien!'"

There is one thing that he is not alien to, and that is hard work. Both of his parents have instilled a strong work ethic into his framework, and his achievements reflect his dedication. It is certainly easy enough to associate other rap stars with drugs, offensive language, misogyny, petty crime, guns, and self-deprecating behavior. Yet, Will Smith has become a sparkling example of what a career in rap music can eventually blossom into. According to him, "While the next guy is sleeping or out at a club, I'm working. A couple of years of that, and I'm going to get a little bit ahead."

No longer content to follow the pack, Smith proudly marches to the beat of a different drummer. Once divorced, he is now married to beautiful actress Jada Pinkett. As the father of two young children, he is very verbal about pre-

Smith with Quincy Jones, the man responsible for producing *The Fresh Prince of Bel Air*.

ferring home life to life with a posse of "homies."

In fact, Will's total disgust with the whole rap music genre caused him to put his recording career on hold right after 1993's *Code Red*. Fortunately, due to the infectious hit theme song from *Men in Black*, he is back to full form with his 1997 solo album, *Big Willie Style*. His 1998 hit single, "Gettin' Jiggy Wit It," has kept him hot on the airwaves as well. Smith is now happily juggling simultaneous careers in

records and films. "I like to do both at different times," he says, explaining his formula. "I enjoy working on movies more in the fall and winter. The spring and summer are more like music times to me. It's a great time to be out doing concerts."

Although he has lived a privileged life, it hasn't been free of self-doubts, pitfalls, controversy, or conflict. In addition to his 1989 near-bankruptcy and taking the heat from frustrated less popular rappers, there were several power

Will and *Men in Black* director Barry Sonnenfeld celebrate the creation of a hit film.

struggles on the set of *The Fresh Prince of Bel Air*, a gay backlash when he refused to kiss another man on camera in *Six Degrees of Separation*, and the bitter resentment of his first marriage turning sour. Fortunately, it has all been met with a very happy ending.

In 1998 he now has a new bride, a new baby, a new Grammy Award, a new hit album, and a new film at the box-office. Still, he remains modest about his triumphant accomplishments. Instead of bragging, he pokes fun at himself. "The secret to my success is that I've got big ears," he laughs. "America needs heroes with large ears. That's why they like me and Mickey Mouse. If they ever do the live-action *Dumbo*, I'm right up there as a contender."

What is the real key to his success? According to Smith himself, "I'm a nice person." Wait a minute, isn't the old proverb "Nice guys always finish last?" Not when it comes to Will Smith. With charm and manners, he has simply rewritten all of the rules.

Smith as Agent Jay in *Men in Black*.

Growing Up in Philly

Will at the beginning of his career as a rapper.

He was born Willard Smith II, on September 25, 1968, in Philadelphia, Pennsylvania. Astrologically, that makes him a Libra, a sign known for their even tempers, elaborate dreams, and a strong sense of creativity. His father, Willard Smith, Sr., at the time was the owner of a refrigeration company, and later became an engineer. His mother, Caroline, worked for the local school board. He was the second child in the Smith household; his appearance followed the birth of his

As the star of TV's *Fresh Prince of Bel Air*.

Will first became a star with the song "Girls Ain't Nothing But Trouble."

child. "He loved to talk," she recalls. "He talked before he could walk."

It was a household that took a lot of pride in the value of education, so that books were an important part of his young education. Growing up, his favorite author was the legendary Dr. Seuss. "If you listen to them a certain way," he says, "books like *Green Eggs and Ham* and *Hop on Pop* sound a lot like hip-hop."

Even from the very beginning Will was the kind of a boy who wanted it all—or-nothing-at-all. "I wasn't the kind of kid who dreamed about being a fireman or policeman," he claims. "I wanted to go up in the space shuttle!"

He always loved music, and wasn't afraid to perform in front of an audience. "There were instruments around the house, and I just played a little of everything," Will says. "Everyone in my family enjoys music, so there was always a lot of music around the house. But my parents made the decisions. If they didn't want me to listen to something, then it didn't happen."

Even the Smith family dinners were entertaining, according to Will. "I was blessed with a really, really funny family. Dinnertime was like a nightly laugh riot," he

older sister, Pam. His other siblings, Harry and Ellen, are twins. To this day, he is still very close to his brother and sisters, and they

work for Will's movie production company.

According to his mother, Will was quite a lively and gregarious claims. "It's always been fun for me to tell a story and make people laugh. I've always been a show-off. I only got uncomfortable when people *weren't* looking at me."

His sister Ellen remembers, "Will did the gross things kids do, like put straws up his nose." She also lovingly recalls, "He always had an energy that drew people to him."

It was at an early age that Will and his siblings received their first taste of stage experience. In fact, it was his own grandmother who was his first casting director. "My grandmother put us all in her little plays at Resurrection Baptist Church," he says.

Although it was an entertaining atmosphere in which to grow up, Will also remembers that his parents were very much in charge, and very strict. According to Will, "My father was a psychotic disciplinarian. My father was in the Air Force, so it was a really military kind of household. . . . Military creases on the bed, all that stuff. . . . I can remember probably five times in my life when my father hit me, because he never really had to: I was so petrified."

Will recalls that even the slightest inference of conflict with his dad was an immediate warning call. He claims that all his father had to say was, "What do you think we could do to assist you in keeping your room clean?" and a tornado-like flurry of Will cleaning his room would instantly occur.

There was no peer pressure that could attempt to top that.

Will attests, "There was no peer pressure that was strong enough to come home and deal with my father. He wanted to make sure that I knew he was my biggest, strongest peer."

For this reason, Will never

His first solo album, *Big Willie Style,* won him a third Grammy Award in 1998.

17

Tyler Collins, Kadeem Hardison, Will Smith, Quincy Jones, and Al B. Sure.

found himself in any sort of trouble during his growing-up years. "Even with peer pressure, there wasn't a friend I had who could pressure me to do something I knew would get me into trouble with my father," he says. "My father had so much control over me when I was growing up—I didn't have too much of an opportunity to do things the wrong way. My father was always in my business. He was always there to make sure I knew what the right way was. He was the man with all the answers, the disciplinarian. He did his shaping up by taking little chunks out of your behind!"

Growing up, Will attended Our Lady of Lourdes, a predominantly white Catholic junior high school. When it came time to attend high school, he then transferred to Overbrook High School, which is mainly black. Looking back on both experiences, Smith explains: "[It was] the best cross section that anybody could have. The first eight years of schooling was with all white people, so that helped me to understand how white people think. I think that transition is what helped me bridge the gap, because that's what my success has really been about: bridging the gap between the black community and the white community."

He claims that he now has the ability to play comedy to both audiences because of his unique background. "Black people enjoy comedy about how the world is," he theorizes. "White people enjoy humor about how the world should be." Will learned an awful lot about comedy during his school years, as he always seemed to be labeled the jokester of every classroom he was in. He especially remembers the school year he turned 12. "I've always been silly," Will says, "but that year was my silliest. I always got in trouble in school for talking, and I was a practical joker. I was definitely the class clown."

Knowing what consequences would occur if his father found out he was pulling off one prank or another, Will simply made certain that he never got caught. "Whenever the teacher was up at the board," he recalls, "I would say something to crack up the entire back of the room. When I saw the teacher start to turn around, my face would go completely blank, like, 'These fractions are so perplexing.' The teacher would go [to another student], 'What's so funny, Jimmy?' And the poor guy didn't even start it, but he was holding the bag."

Will's father taught him how to play the classic board game of strategy, chess, when young Will was only eight years old. It wasn't until the time he was 14 that he was finally able to win a game. "I saw the checkmate coming," he recalls, "and I was petrified. It built my self-esteem."

His sense of self-confidence comes from a very honest place within him. He claims, "There's a certain level of confidence and self-esteem that comes from knowing for a fact that someone loves you. It's not based on whether or not I break a window; it's not based on whether or not my homework's done. Just because I'm me, these people love me. So, it's like, I know I'm good. How can I let the world know?"

He also knew that if anything bad happened to him, he could always depend on his family to look out for him. "I was nine and my older sister must have been 15," he says of one such incident. "Some guys pulled a knife on me and took my money when I was coming home from school. I came in crying and my sister asked me why. I told her and she right away grabbed a baseball bat. We walked around for four hours looking for this guy. She had no concern for her own safety. Somebody had done something to her brother and she was going to do everything in her power to make sure they never did it again. We never found the guys, but that type of love and commitment is what I search for."

He also had a very vivid imagination, and as a child he was fascinated by dinosaurs. Specifically, he loved the stegosaurus. When he reached the age of 12, his focus was on arithmetic and numbers. "I guess they seemed definite, you know, like something you could latch on to. A fact."

According to Will, drugs were never an option for him, even though they were certainly plentiful in the city of Philadelphia. "I'm so silly I never felt a need for substances," he laughs.

One day when Will was still a kid, Willard Smith, Sr., took him for a ride in the car to some skid row street to teach him a lesson about life. "He pointed to the bums sleeping in the doorways and said, 'This is what people

Will Smith, his son Trey, and his first wife, Sheree, in 1994.

Will is the center of attention, with the cast of *The Fresh Prince of Bel Air.*

look like when they do drugs,'" Will recalls. It was a lesson he never forgot.

One summer, their father had Will and brother Harry tear down a brick wall, and put it back together again. It took them the entire summer, but when they were finished they were impressed by what they had accomplished with their own hard work. "Now, don't ever tell me you can't do something. Then I think about that wall, and tell myself, 'One brick at a time.'"

Will's brother, Harry, with whom Will shared a bedroom, recalls, "He used to bum around everywhere. And I always remember his feet used to stink. My mom would make him wash his feet." Spoken like a true younger brother.

When asked in the press who his childhood idols were, Will truthfully replied, "There are individual personality traits of celebrities and sports stars I admire, but the only people I continue to idolize are my parents. They taught me clearly the difference between right and wrong, and that when you make a mistake, you must be honest with yourself about it."

If he did have a show business idol growing up, he admits that it was Eddie Murphy. At the time Eddie was one of the stars of *Saturday Night Live*, and in the early 1980s was just beginning to break into movies. "Eddie is a genius," Will declares. "That was something I instinctively knew."

It was the school year he turned 13 that Will Smith heard something which was to have a tremendous effect on his life. "I started listening to rap records in the summer after seventh grade. That's when I bought one of my first rap records, *Rapper's Delight* by the Sugar Hill Gang."

Explains Will, "When you grow up in any urban area, particularly a black area, you can't escape it. Rap is the urban music.

Everybody on the street is a rapper, or a D.J., or a beat box. Hip-hop is culture. It's not just music, it's a way of life."

He had never been much of a singer, but suddenly he had found a musical genre which fit him to a tee. "My voice is definitely not a singing voice. Rap music came along at a perfect time for me," he proclaims.

"I started rapping just as soon as I heard that first song. I rapped all day long until I thought my mom was going to lose her mind! Music, after all, has always been in my heart. At first, I did it as a hobby, and I enjoyed it and got really good at it. When you enjoy what you do, you're going to get really good at it. And I just concentrated on it."

He started rapping wherever he went, whether it was at parties, dances, or out on the street. "My reputation came from beating other rappers in street challenges. I never lost a street battle," he claims. Although he didn't realize it at the time, it was rap music that was going to change his life.

Will and Tommy Lee Jones in *Men in Black*.

D.J. Jazzy Jeff & the Fresh Prince

It wasn't long before Will Smith had really perfected his rapping style, and his knowledge of how to "scratch" records on the turntable. "I started off as a D.J.," he explains. "My parents bought me turntables and drove me to parties and church functions, so I could D.J. I began rapping as a hobby, and it grew into a career."

He found himself getting better and better at it all the time. "I was going to all those block par-

While he was still a teenager, Will was nicknamed the Fresh Prince.

With Jeff Townes, as D.J. Jazzy Jeff & the Fresh Prince.

Jeff and Will built up a strong reputation for rocking the house in their native Philadelphia, and then they turned their music into an international sensation.

At this time, Will truly felt that it was his family life, and the strength of it, that kept him together. However, when Will was 13 years old, his parents sat their children down and explained very calmly that they were getting a divorce. Looking back on this time in his life, Will claims, "You can't spring off into the world from a flimsy base, you've got to have a solid base to jump from. My parents, together or apart, provided that base."

Although the Smith family no longer lived under the same roof, both his father and his mother continued to take an active role in their children's upbringing. Thankfully, Will and his brothers and sisters were old enough to realize that both of their parents loved them very much, and the situation didn't compromise either their mother's love or their father's love for them.

Meanwhile, in another part of Philadelphia there was a young man by the name of Jeff Townes, who was destined to play a very important part in Will Smith's life. He possessed the same passion for rap music that Will had.

"When rap came out, there was a buzz: *This* is something new!" Jeff recalls. "We never heard this before, but somebody

ties, having fun and competing with my raps. It suddenly occurred to me, 'Okay, if I'm going to party, I might as well get paid for it,'" he says.

"What my father always made very clear to me is just do one thing well, just make sure you can focus.

If you do one thing well, everything else will come from that. I started off rapping, and I did it as a hobby. And that's when you really get good at something. When you enjoy what you do, you're gonna get good at it. And I just really concentrated on it, and I focused on it."

The Fresh Prince and Jazzy Jeff at the beginning of their rap music career.

made this especially for us. This is *our* music because our parents don't like it, our grandmothers don't like it. But *we* like it."

He rehearsed spinning and scratching records, and became quite adept as a disk jockey. "I used to call myself a bathroom D.J.," Townes explains, "because I would tag along to parties with older D.J.s and finally get my chance to go on when they went to the bathroom!"

It wasn't long before Jeff had a local reputation. According to

him, "I was the best D.J. in Philadelphia and I had heard of Will, but I already had someone that I worked with. But when I played that party on Will's block, naturally he was there. He asked if he could rap for a while and I said yes. He started rapping and I started cutting, and it was like natural chemistry. He flowed with what I did and I flowed exactly with what he did and we knew it. We just clicked the whole night long. The chemistry between us was so good. I went home and

dreamed about him. I got his number and we got together."

The pair had met at the neighborhood park in January of 1986, and it wasn't long before Jeff Townes and Will Smith began to really mesh as a team: D.J. and rapper. All they needed was a stage identity to complete the act. With his love of jazz music, Jeff Townes easily slipped into the persona of D.J. Jazzy Jeff. For a while Will Smith's friends and family had referred to him as "Prince," for his aristocratic way of carrying

"I don't understand groups who come on stage looking real mad. We just want people to have fun."

himself. Since the word "fresh" was a hot superlative circa 1987, it seemed like "Fresh Prince" was a natural moniker for him.

Explaining his use of the word "fresh" at the time, Will says, "It was street talk for cool, the best." And, the "best" was what he aimed to become.

From the minute that they became dubbed "D.J. Jazzy Jeff & the Fresh Prince," Jeff and Will were inseparable. Not only did they become instant friends on stage and off, but they soon learned that they both shared a silly sense of humor. According to Jeff, "A few weeks after we met, we were working a party together. I bought this canned fart spray called PU, and as a goof, sprayed it at the party. I cracked up, and so did Will. That's when I realized we were down with the same humor. That's when we really clicked."

After he started writing rap lyrics, Will recalls that his grandmother discovered his writing pad one day, and was appalled by what she read. She, in turn, picked up a pen and piece of paper and wrote him a letter. In the letter, in her meticulous grandmother's penmanship, she wrote him a list of every dirty word she never wanted to hear coming out of his mouth. When Will received the letter, he nearly freaked out. First of all, he had no idea those words were even in his grandmother's vocabulary. From that point on, all of Will's raps have been characterized by the fact that they don't contain a single word of profanity, nor do they glorify drugs, guns, or violence.

While the majority of rap songs at the time featured demeaning lyrics about pimps, "ho's" (whores), "bitches," drugs, guns, petty crime, and macho bravado, sung with a misogynistic slant, Jeff and Will began to take little snippets, or "samples," of popular songs, and they rewrote amusing new lyrics that reflected their crazy sense of humor. Then they set it all off to a snappy rap beat.

The fact that their raps were 100 percent clean, and yet amusing and entertaining at the same time, became the trademark of D.J. Jazzy Jeff & the Fresh Prince. Jeff claims that it wasn't long before they came to realize: "Together, we could be the ultimate, not just in Philadelphia, but everywhere. Nobody could touch us."

Will proudly explains, "We had a pretty new style that people were finding interesting. Plus, we could make people laugh at a party scene."

Also, by the time he was a young teenager, Will Smith was growing into quite a handsome young man. It wasn't long before he wouldn't have to rely upon his reputation as "class clown" to get people's attention. Will also learned that fronting a musical act was a sure way to attract the girls. However, that doesn't mean that he was a natural-born Casanova either. "My first sexual experience never really, like, got off the ground," he sheepishly admits. "It was with my girlfriend in eighth grade. Gosh, I shouldn't have said that—I mean my girlfriend in eleventh grade, Mom! Anyway, it happened at my house and all, but it just took me, like 30 minutes to figure out how to get the rubber to work—sorry, Mom, the prophylactic. I just didn't know how to work it. It was dark, too, and I dropped it and then I had to turn the lights on to find it. Anyway, finally it really didn't . . . uhmm . . . happen, because I got a little ahead of myself—so to speak." Even Don Juan, literature's fabled lover, must have had an awkward teenage phase with the opposite sex as well!

Now that he was using his sense of humor in his rapping, Will was really flexing his sense of humor in front of anyone who would listen to him. He especially remembers ninth grade at Over-brook High School as the height of his "class clown" phase. "I was just silly all the time," he says. "People I went to school with probably remember me as a jack-ass. I always used to get into silly trouble, but I was always so charming, I could smooth talk my way out of any situation."

During this era, although he wasn't into school per se, he still maintained a strong grade point average. "I got the grades mainly to please my parents," he says in retrospect. "I didn't think I'd ever use what I leaned. But in my rap and as an actor, it's amazing how much of what I did learn comes back to me. It all pays off in the end. I just didn't know that then."

Jazzy Jeff & the Fresh Prince were known for rap music that contained no profanity. It was just fun music, and it sold like hotcakes.

There was a lot of controversy surrounding Will and Jeff at the start of their career. Other rappers found their sense of humor too silly and irreverent.

From the very beginning, they had grandiose dreams of fame. "Our destiny was to be the most versatile group to come out of rap," Will and Jeff both claimed. "We'd sit down and talk about things first. The songs come from our own experiences."

Since they were a pair of middle-class boys from strong disciplinary homes, Will and Jeff's initial hit record came directly from the pages of their own personal journals—it was a song called "Girls Ain't Nothing But Trouble." Instead of demeaning women,

the song amusingly tells the woes of dating from a teenager's standpoint, with hysterically funny results. To top it all off—just to complete the sense of goofiness of the humorous tune—the whole song is set to a "sample" of the musical theme from the 1960s hit television show *I Dream of Jeannie*. Instead of pony-tailed Barbara Eden popping out of an Arabian vase, the girls that Will sings about in his rap get this homeboy teenager into one embarrassing fix after another. Will's advice in the lyrics of the song call for all men to "get the hell away" whenever approached by women, because he has discovered that "Girls Ain't Nothing But Trouble."

Will and Jeff were so certain that the song was a hit that they recorded a version of it and submitted it to Dana Goodman of Word Up Records. Much to everyone's surprise, they were instantly offered a one-shot recording deal. "Girls Ain't Nothing But Trouble" became one of the biggest rap records on both sides of the Atlantic Ocean, going Top 20 in Great Britain, selling over 100,000 copies.

However, things were less than optimal amidst their tenure at Word Up Records. According to Smith, "I've been in really ugly situations, hostage situations, on the road with my music. You know, you get out to Albany, Georgia, and the promoter didn't make his money, so he doesn't want to pay you. I mean, during the first part of my music career, we signed our first deal with a gangster who later tried to shoot us. He was a penny-ante gangster, but the bullets were for real. As we were driving away, he shot at the car five or six times. It was pretty scary, but you don't think about that while it's happening, you're just trying to get away. He would have killed us if he could actually shoot."

The summer following the release of "Girls Ain't Nothing But Trouble," D.J. Jazzy Jeff & the Fresh Prince joined LL Cool J, Eric B. & Rakim, Whodini, and Public Enemy, and they were all flown to England as part of a Def Jam Records tour of the British Isles. Unbeknownst to Will and Jeff, their debut record had made a much bigger impression on the record-buying public in England than it did in their own country. Will recalls, "There were screaming girls at the airport, and we just thought, 'What is this? What are they screaming for?'" This was only the beginning.

In addition to becoming an instant hit, the song "Girls Ain't

Nothing But Trouble" also tipped off quite a controversy in the rap community as well as in the press. First of all they took some heat for "dissing" women in their song. Secondly, several members of the rap community began making public statements about Jeff and Will making fun of rap music. In reality, it sounds like a case of jealousy.

"That's a ridiculous, idiotic opinion," Will proclaimed at the time. "The rap is a personal story, told with a sense of humor, rather than a statement of general attitude." When it came time to record their first album, *Rock the House*, Jeff and Will moved over to Jive Records. On that record they included a version of their first hit

song, which was a duet with female rapper, Ice Cream Tee, on the "answer song" entitled "Guys Ain't Nothing But Trouble!"

The album *Rock the House* contained further forays into tongue-in-cheek rap music, including the song "Just One of Those Days," which is set to a sample of Irving Berlin's "Puttin' on the Ritz." On the song "Don't Even Try It," Will took time to "diss" their detractors. He raps about a girl named Teresa who wouldn't give him the time of day until he had a hit record, then she was suddenly phoning him. His answer to her was naturally: "Don't Even Try It."

The duo was so amazed even to have an album deal, they used one whole cut on *Rock the House*, entitled "Special Announcement," just to thank everyone who had helped them along the way. Based on the hit recording "Girls Ain't Nothing But Trouble," when the album was released it became a huge hit, and established them as one of the most successful rap groups in the recording business.

That alone became a slight problem, because all of this excitement in the record business took

After Jeff and Will recorded the song "Parents Just Don't Understand," they were livin' large.

"The rap is a personal story, told with a sense of humor, rather than a statement of general attitude."

place during Will's senior year in high school. His parents were expecting him to go on to college as he had always planned. His sudden success as a rap artist had begun to take its toll on his grades. "My guidance counselor called my mom and told her that I was testing at college level, but my grades did not reflect it," he recalls. "I had really high SAT scores."

There had been some talk about Will going to Massachusetts Institute of Technology (MIT), the educational institution depicted in the 1997 film *Good Will Hunting*. According to Will, "I was talking to the guys [college recruiters] from MIT, and there was some kind of two-year pre-engineering prep course that they were interested in having me apply for."

However, when he told his mother "This guy at MIT sounds really nice, but I want to be a rapper. I think I can do that," he recalls. "She had a conniption. She let me talk to my father, who

was also not too thrilled with the course of events. Still, my father basically said, 'Okay. Take a year. If it works, God bless you. If it doesn't, you'll go to college.'"

That effectively ended Will's college aspirations. He and Jeff returned to the recording studio, and never looked back once.

In 1988 D.J. Jazzy Jeff & the Fresh Prince released a vinyl two-record set called *He's The D.J., I'm The Rapper.* It contained two of their biggest hits, "Nightmare On My Street" and "Parents Just Don't Understand." The first song, set to a horror movie theme, is a rap tribute to the Freddie Kruger *Nightmare on Elm Street* slasher movies. However, it was "Parents Just Don't Understand" that truly cemented everything for them.

Not only did it become a huge hit on the Black Music charts in America, it also became a monster hit on pop stations across the country, programmed in between cuts by Debbie Gibson and by

Tiffany. When MTV caught the equally humorous video of D.J. Jazzy Jeff & the Fresh Prince and put it on "heavy rotation," the record sold like hotcakes—not only to black record buyers, but to white record buyers as well. Defending the song's humorous theme, Will said in a perplexed voice, "I don't understand groups who come on stage looking real mad. We just want people to have fun."

This was all it took for a huge controversy to ensue. Amongst the duo's biggest detractors was rapper Big Daddy Kane. In an accusatory statement, Kane knocked D.J. Jazzy Jeff & the Fresh Prince for creating rap music for white people.

Will Smith came out fighting and blasted his critic by proclaiming, "I don't think anyone can dictate what's black and what's not black. Big Daddy Kane is ignorant and doesn't realize what black really means. He thinks being articulate is being white. We're trying to show the world, and black kids, that you can dress nicely and speak well and still be considered black. Our music is black music. Our families are black, we came from black backgrounds."

He furthermore stated, "We're going to continue to rap about things we have experienced. Not only that, lots of people can relate to us. In 'Parents Just Don't Understand,' we wanted to write about something everybody could relate to. I wasn't trying to appeal to a white audience, or do any-thing different. I was writing about what I related to, what I thought was interesting. It's from my own experience."

The brilliant thing about "Parents Just Don't Understand" is the fact that it amusingly expressed an experience that every teenage kid—black or white or yellow or red or brown—could identify with. It centered around going to the local shopping mall with your parents, and standing by in absolute horror while they proceed to pick out the most uncool outfits to dress you in.

According to Smith, "We do rap from a different point of view. We make it fun. We make it universal. My point of view isn't limited. It's very broad. It's more than the black experience. . . . We are humorous, we like to have fun. We let our personalities run through our work. Both of us have a good sense of humor and we don't act any differently when we make a record. You don't have to come on rough to rap. If there's funny stuff on our album, it comes from us . . . I would never do anything that my mother couldn't turn on her radio and listen to. I would never do anything to offend my family."

Even his own mother came out in her son's defense. "This

Jazzy Jeff & the Fresh Prince at Disneyland.

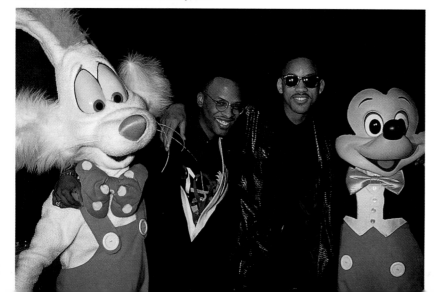

album's good, even I can stand to listen to it," she publicly proclaimed.

"Why do you have to compare D.J. Jazzy Jeff & the Fresh Prince with other rappers? Rap is just like any other kind of music. You can't compare Luther Vandross to Michael Jackson, so why do we have to be compared to Public Enemy or Tone-Loc? All rap is real," Will insisted.

In January of 1989 D.J. Jazzy Jeff & the Fresh Prince made a clean sweep at the *American Music Awards* telecast, capturing trophies in the categories of "Best Artist" and "Best Album" for *He's The D.J., I'm The Rapper*. The following month, "Parents Just Don't Understand" made history when it became the first recording to win the very first Grammy in the newly created category of "Best Rap Single."

Suddenly, while still a teenager, Will Smith was rolling in money. Speaking at the time about the recent success that rap music was experiencing, he proclaimed, "The music is good. It's realistic. It's here. Mainstream businessmen and industry are opening up."

Drinking in the first taste of success, Will and Jeff went a little nuts with the spending. Like so many people in show business

Jeff and Will in the winner's circle at The Grammy Awards, February 1998.

who experience their first bit of monetary success, there is an illusion that money will always continue to flow as freely. A false sense of security sets in, and the spending becomes out of control.

Now that they were a huge hit, they suddenly had a huge entourage of friends. When it came time to record their third album, they rented rock star Robert Palmer's villa in Compass Point in the Bahamas, which comes complete with full recording facilities. Just so they could continue to party, they then flew all of their friends and cronies to

the Bahamas with them, expenses paid. In twelve days, they recorded four new songs for their upcoming album. Will's logic at the time was, "We have to record—why not go someplace exciting to do it?"

He didn't realize at the time what was happening to him. All he knew was that he had more money in his bank account than he had ever seen before. In his own defense he explained, "I'm pretty much the same person. Success hasn't changed me much. Now the difference is, I can get two burgers instead of one."

Even his own mother came out in her son's defense. "This album's good. Even I can stand to listen to it."

To top it all off, Jeff and Will decided to start their own "hotline" for their fans to get tour information, and to hear a recorded message from Jazzy Jeff & the Fresh Prince. By dialing the number, their fans were also charged an average of $2.45 a call. After they advertised the 1-900-909-JEFF line in their 1989 *And In This Corner* album, even more money poured in. That's when the trouble really escalated.

"One year I spent $800,000. I went through it so fast, it made my head spin. Being able to buy anything you want makes you a little crazy," Will recalls. He went completely out-of-control with his spending. First there were the cars and other vehicles, seven in all, including a Corvette, a truck, a Suzuki motorbike, a bright red Camaro, and a Suburban station wagon—complete with a 2,200-watt stereo system for rapping down the highway. Then there was the solid gold necklace spelling out the words "Fresh Prince" in sparkling diamonds. To top it all off came the mansion. In the tiny neighborhood of Merion, in the Philadelphia suburbs, young Will Smith was "livin' large" in his own princely castle of a home.

Just in case his buddies stopped by, Will also had to have a well-stocked party pad. At the time he described his kitchen as "looking like a mini-mart with rows of bottled juice in the cabinets and dozens of cuts of meat in the freezer."

"Even if it was ugly, I bought it," he claims. "Once I flew to London and Tokyo just to buy clothes." One day while in Atlanta with his posse of buddies, he called ahead to the local Gucci designer store, and commanded them to "Close it, we're coming." He later admitted, "It was a power trip."

No one was more appalled with this flagrant display of excess than his own father. "He saw me blowing money that could allow me to set myself up for the rest of my life," Will recalls.

It wasn't long after that he learned that all that glistens is not always golden. "I spent a long time trying to figure out how things could be going so well, and I could be so unhappy."

Will Smith seemed to have it all. He was a big star in the record business, he owned his own house, he had a circle of friends whom he paid to have around him; it seemed like it would never end. However he forgot about one important detail: putting aside money for the income tax bill. One day he heard from the IRS, and it seemed like it was all over. What he owed the government in back taxes was reportedly in the millions. Suddenly the non-stop party ended.

"There was nothing funny about it," Will says nowadays. "It was a matter of being young, wild, and stupid. But there was nothing anyone could have done. At that age, with that amount of money, it's difficult to handle. And because I was eighteen, the checks came to me, so it was difficult for anyone to intervene in the ludicrous behavior I was displaying. Besides, I didn't listen to anyone. Everything my parents taught me was out the window as soon as that cash hit the bank account."

What was most amazing was the speed at which everything suddenly fell apart around him. "Being able to buy anything you want makes you a little crazy," he says in retrospect. "I learned my lesson, though. One day I had six cars and a mansion; the next, I couldn't pay the gas bill. I had to change my attitude. I won't ever make that mistake again."

Happily, he is now able to look back at this period in his life from a more enlightened space. "I had a period in my life where I sought attention, had a little money, and wanted to flex it all. But the real person inside me eventually dictated how I had to act, how I had to behave, and how I had to treat people. My parents and my upbringing weighed out over the temptation of the glitter, the money, and all that. Who I really am wins every time," he admits. Ultimately, that was just what was destined to happen.

Will went wild with spending in the late 1980s, purchasing things he couldn't afford, like this diamond-studded solid gold Fresh Prince necklace he wears in the company of Karyn Parsons.

Fresh Prince of Bel Air

It was a bitter pill to swallow, but as the new decade began, Will Smith was behind the eight ball. He was massively in debt, and the last album, *And In This Corner,* had failed to feature a hit anywhere nearly as big as "Parents Just Don't Understand." According to Will, "In 1990, I was dealing with the decline in my music—at least in my eyes. I was looking for something new, something else to do." Somehow, from out of the depths of depression, Will was about to experience a huge windfall of good luck.

Enter: Benny Medina. At the time, Benny was 31 years old, and a vice president in the Black Music department of Warner Brothers Records in Los Angeles. Medina had come from a poor family in East L.A. When he was still a kid, his mother died, and he had no relatives who were able to take care of him. At the age of 15 he was placed in a foster home. The home just happened to be in wealthy Beverly Hills, California. The family who took him in was well-to-do TV and film composer Jack Elliot. Elliot, his wife, and his three children became Benny's new family. The family happened to be white, so this was completely foreign to Medina's previous experiences in life.

He moved into the Elliots' garage, which had been converted into an apartment for him. To have gone from being an underprivileged black teenager with no hope and no future, to suddenly living in Beverly Hills, was like Cinderella must have felt after she found that the glass slipper fit her foot perfectly.

According to Medina, "My

Will's acting career began with him as the star of TV's *Fresh Prince of Bel Air.*

deal was that I had to maintain good grades, keep a job, and respect the household. I was kind of an aggressive, smart-ass kid coming into a place where they had such a completely different background. I could never figure out how I was going to exist in that household."

It just so happened that the Elliots' list of friends also included Frank Sinatra, Dean Martin, and the president of legendary Motown Records—Berry Gordy, Jr. According to Medina, "I literally put on a backpack and rode my bike to their home in Beverly Hills. I never left." Benny was living a virtual rags-to-riches story. It was such an amazing story in fact, that Medina long harbored the idea that this fortunate twist of fate would make the perfect TV series.

It was another strange twist of fate in 1990 that threw Benny and Will Smith together. They were both at a taping of the popular TV variety program *The Arsenio Hall Show.* That particular day Hall was taping a special episode to honor record producer Quincy Jones.

Benny instantly hit it off with

The Fresh Prince clowning with his uncle and aunt, portrayed by James Avery and Janet Hubert.

Smith, and he confessed that he had this great idea for a television series. A light went off in Medina's head. Will Smith would be perfect as the star of the series; now all he needed was a producer—someone powerful in the entertainment business—someone like Quincy Jones. That day was the day that the ball began rolling toward what was to become one of the most popular network television series of the 1990s, *The Fresh Prince of Bel Air*.

Quincy loved the idea, and he procured some tapes of Will Smith on camera, appearing on the show *Yo! MTV Raps*. He played them for the head of NBC Entertainment, Brandon Tartikoff, and NBC network chief Warren Littlefield. They liked the idea. Medina mentioned that he knew a black Beverly Hills family who had lived in the Elliots' neighborhood, and how different their existence was as black Americans, compared to what he had previously known. Along the way, a decision was made to change the adopting family from white to black, and to market the show primarily toward the black TV-viewing audience.

All that was needed to really start the show off was a strong star to carry the series. To accomplish this task, Quincy Jones

In the Philadelphia suburbs, young Will Smith was "livin' large" in his own princely castle of a home.

invited several key executives from NBC-TV to his plush home in Bel Air, California to meet Will Smith, and for him to audition. With a sample script, Will memorized his lines and prepared for the audition that was to change his life.

Warren Littlefield recalls that day very distinctly. According to him, Will was very nervous. "There were beads of sweat [on his forehead]," he claims, "But Will read from a script and just nailed it. I sat there thinking, 'Whoa! Just bottle this guy!'"

According to Benny, "Will put some of his personal nuances in, and right after that, everybody was shaking hands, hugging and kissing."

In very rapid succession, a deal was cut, producers and writers were hired, and preparations were made to put *The Fresh Prince of Bel Air* into production for a fall 1990 debut. According to the new version of the show,

the Fresh Prince goes to Bel Air to live with his Aunt Vivian and his Uncle Phil Banks and their children in their affluent home.

James Avery was cast as Uncle Phillip, and Janet Hubert-Whitten portrayed Aunt Vivian. Their children were played by Karyn Parsons as Hilary Banks, Alfonso Ribeiro as Carlton Banks, and 12-year-old Tatyana M. Ali as Ashley Banks. The role of their butler, Geoffrey, was portrayed by Joseph Marcell.

This was the chance of a lifetime, and Will knew it. At the time he proclaimed, "What I am the happiest about is that I can be a role model and give people something to think about. It's important to have a black show that's positive. Television has been controlled by white America and they've had a tendency to put their own on."

He also admitted that there was a great deal of pressure placed on him. "There was kind of a concern about the unknown," he recalls. "I was one of the first of the hip-hop generation on television, so there was a sense of wonder if it was going to translate, about how America would accept this hip-hoppin', be-boppin', fast-talking kind of black guy."

There were, however,

moments where he wondered if he was going to fall flat on his face. "I was wondering at the beginning why no one ever asked if I could act. Not Quincy, not NBC. Nobody. They even shot the pilot and never asked me, 'Can you act?'"

Yet, in true schizophrenic Libra tradition, he also felt confi-

dent that he was up to the challenge. "I have a pretty good eye and ear for what America will think is funny. [However], this is the only acting I've ever done," he claimed.

After the pilot episode was taped, it was shown to the network brass, and they loved it. Everyone felt that Will Smith was a natural performer who had a huge future in front of him. However, when he viewed his first work on camera, he freaked out. He absolutely hated what he saw. "There were things I could have done better. I missed the rhythm, I didn't quite hit the laughs."

Will had some self-doubts. "I sucked. Badly. I can't believe how many mistakes I made," he later confessed. "I was trying so hard. I would memorize the entire script, then I'd be mouthing everybody's lines right back at them—while they were talking. When I watch those [first] episodes, it's disgusting. My performances were horrible."

Tatyana Ali, who played the role of his little sister was later to proclaim, "I couldn't believe what a bad actor he was. I'd do a scene with him and he would mouth my words while I was doing my lines . . . If you look at the old shows, you can see it."

In his own defense, Will was

later to explain, "I was afraid of missing my lines."

Yet, when the show debuted in September of 1990, it was a huge hit, with audiences and with the press as well. The *New York Times* proclaimed, "One initial doubt about the program has already been resolved, however: Mr. Smith not only can sing, write, and dance, he clearly can act too." And the reviewer in *TV Guide* concurred, "Will Smith's enjoyment of his role is infectious."

To top it all off, the people who were responsible for producing the show began to rave about what an incredible actor Will was. Quincy Jones sincerely stated, "I know real stars. I've worked with Streisand, Sinatra, Michael Jackson. Will Smith has the same potential to climb to the same heights as those greats. He's a monster talent."

Will did admit that he improved that season as time went by, but he still didn't feel that he was really connecting with the audience, or was on top of his game. Although he worked very hard in this trial-by-fire television show, he was later to lament, "The only thing that saved me on the show that first year was that everybody else in the cast was

NBC TV executive Brandon Tartikoff and *Fresh Prince* stars Will Smith, Karyn Parsons, and Alfonso Ribiero.

funny."

One had to admit that Will sure looked and sounded great on camera that first season. He was being hypercritical of himself, but inside he was striving for perfection, and a performance that showed him off as being the best he could be.

Tatyana Ali recalls, "Will always got his hair cut every Friday morning before the [taping of the] show, and was really particular about getting it shaped the right way."

For the most part, the set of the TV show had a family atmos-

phere. However, even families aren't without their conflicts. According to Will, "That first year Tatyana and I clashed because I felt like her older brother, and she wasn't having any of it."

The odd thing was that people either loved his performances on *The Fresh Prince of Bel Air* or they hated them. On the "love him" side of the fence was the top brass at NBC-TV. Some very influential people even started comparing him to Eddie Murphy in their interviews with the press. When NBC's Brandon Tartikoff did it, Will complained, "People are

> **He was determined to become the best actor he could be, no matter what it took, and he wasn't going to let up until he reached his goal.**

expecting a lot, and I've never done any acting, so I don't want to be compared to anyone. I have a natural feel, but let me practice first so I can be proud of what I do."

On the other side of the coin, Will continued to be publicly "dissed" and trashed by hard-core rappers for his easygoing and articulate style on television. He blasted back by stating, "I have a lot of opinions. I agree with things that Chuck D and Public Enemy say, but I have a different way of expressing myself. I like blending a message with comedy so it's subtle. I want people to enjoy themselves, then be left with something subliminally."

Will's first year in Los Angeles wasn't one of wild partying or extravagances. He was just so glad to be out of debt to the IRS that he was content to become a home-

body completely dedicated to his craft. When members of the media asked him why he didn't hang out on Sunset Strip, he replied. "I'm an in-house type of person. I'm not out at the clubs and anything like that. I just don't hang out with too many new people."

According to him, "I don't need a social life. I've got to work now, and I'll have a social life when I'm thirty. I'm not into the L.A. lifestyle anyway. It takes your mind off work."

Simultaneously, he and Jazzy Jeff were working on cuts for their fourth album, *Homebase*. It was like holding two jobs at once. He said at the time, "I'm doing the show from nine to five, and from six to midnight, I'm in the studio working on the album. But as long as I get my eight hours of sleep, I'm fine."

So that Jeff had a reason to be

with Will in Los Angles beyond recording the album, Will made sure that he was used in a recurring role on *The Fresh Prince of Bel Air*. After a year of financial terror, both he and Jeff were riding a big wave of newfound success. It was like Smith had been given a second chance, after making a harrowing mistake with his finances.

Will was also very aware that he had the opportunity of a lifetime to be starring in his own television show. However, instead of resting on his laurels, he was determined to improve his acting skills, and to make sure the show was as strong and popular as possible. He wasn't buying all of the compliments that were being lauded upon him. According to him at the time, "Nobody knows what a runaway hit is until the fans say it's a runaway hit."

According to him, "My motivation is that I hate not being on top. I get mad by being creative." He was determined to become the best actor he could be, no matter what it took, and he wasn't going to let up until he reached his goal.

Will and boxer Evander Hollafield on *The Fresh Prince of Bel Air*.

42

Will Breaks into Films

Once Will lived through the first season of *The Fresh Prince of Bel Air* and completed the *Homebase* album, he caught his breath and centered himself enough to get his confidence and his energies focused. While the rap world continued to pump out albums full of negative messages, Will and Jeff delivered a fourth dose of positive tunes. The album's biggest hit single, "Summertime," went on to win Jazzy Jeff & the Fresh Prince their second Grammy Award.

Will in *Made in America*.

Will in his first film role, as Manny in *Where the Day Takes You*.

Gaining more confidence in everything he was involved in, Will was ready to take on some new challenges. His next big goal was to break into the movies. For so many of the hottest actors on the big screen, their hit television series proved to become their stepping stones to a bigger and greater career. Robin Williams had gotten his start on *Mork and Mindy* in the mid-'70s. Tom Hanks had his first taste of success in the series *Bosom Buddies*. Eddie Murphy first became popular as one of the regular actors on *Saturday Night Live*. Now Will too wanted to make the transition from the small screen to the big screen.

Recalls *Fresh Prince* creator Benny Medina, "Movies were something he said he wanted to do the first time we talked to him. Within the next couple of days, he had to do an audition, and he picked up this lousy script and read life into lines he had never seen before in front of the network brass and everyone. Afterward, I realized I had just sat through one of those moments that people always talk about having. Once he was in front of the camera, he still had the ability to completely capture your attention and really hold it."

When the recording duo of Kid 'N Play became the first rappers to star in their own movie, *House Party*, Will said, "The characters they play are from their everyday lives. I think the music and the culture of rap breed an aura of honesty and realism that people can relate to. That's why it

Ted Danson, Whoopi Goldberg, and Will Smith in *Made In America*.

Dermot Mulroney, Ricki Lake, James LeGros, Balthazar Getty, Will Smith, Sean Austin, and Laura Flynn Boyle as kids who live on the streets of Los Angeles in *Where the Day Takes You*.

translates to the screen well."

Will was anxious and ready to get in front of the movie cameras the minute *Where the Day Takes You* came along. It was a low-budget film, made prestigious by the first-rate cast who starred in it: Dermot Mulroney [*My Best Friend's Wedding*], Sean Austin, Balthazar Getty, Ricki Lake, Lara Flynn Boyle, Kyle McLaughlin, Nancy McKeon, Adam Baldwin, Alyssa Milano, and Laura San Giacomo, plus Christian Slater in an unbilled role. It is the grim story of a bunch of runaway kids on the streets of Los Angeles,

strung out on drugs, and living their lives in a harrowing, dead-end fashion. It is the story of King (Dermot Mulroney) who gets out of jail only to find his life in shambles. As part of his parole, he must see a therapist regularly, and the story he spins becomes the movie that unfolds. Large portions of it are shot in a very grainy documentary-like fashion.

Will portrays Manny, a legless street boy with a goatee. He lives on his wheelchair on Hollywood Boulevard, begging for money on the streets. The film gave Will the opportunity to really lose himself

in a dramatic role, and what is seen on camera is a very anti-type role for Will. One of his motivations for taking the role in this grim and gritty movie was simply to get some legitimate acting credentials under his belt. He has a small part at the beginning of the film, then two other scenes.

Kyle McLaughlin is great as a sleazy drug dealer who shoots up between his toes, and Ricki Lake seems to constantly be eating her way through the movie on either pizza or ketchup-coated French fries. And, Will was able to gain a lot of confidence in front of the

One of the best parts about filming *Made in America* was working with Whoopi Goldberg.

movie camera. He soon found that film acting was a lot different than the broader way of acting that television comedy requires.

In his second scene, Will is shown on his wheelchair, begging on Hollywood Boulevard and accosting passersby. In his third and last scene, he is dragged into a dark alley by a thug, and is pushed over onto the concrete.

One of the most interesting things that Will learned from this experience had nothing to do with acting, but everything with life on the street. According to him, "Just seeing how people ignore the homeless was an amazing lesson. I was in full make-up on Hollywood Boulevard, and people didn't know me. It was a revelation seeing how cold people can be."

While continuing to work on a full season of *The Fresh Prince of Bel Air* the following year, Will appeared in the 1993 hit comedy *Made in America*, directed by comedy expert Richard Benjamin. The plot centers around Nia Long, who portrays the daughter of Whoopi Goldberg. When she presses her mother to disclose the identity of her long-missing dad, Whoopi has to confess to her that she had gone to a sperm bank to father her child. When Nia insists upon tracking down her birth father, she and Whoopi are shocked to find that the sperm donor is in fact a white man, played by Ted Danson. In addition to being white, he turns out to be the well-known owner of a local Los Angeles used-car lot, who on television is seen in his own ads, coming across as a loutish buffoon.

In the film Will Smith plays the part of Tea Cake Walters, Nia's friend and schoolmate. Although they have been best friends for years, Smith's character is deeply in love with Nia. Although Will's part in the movie wasn't one of the pivotal roles, he was one of the film's stars, and it provided him with the chance to be seen in an A-list film. To top it all off, *Made in America* was a huge box-office success, grossing over $100 million dollars.

According to Smith, "Working with Whoopi was really cool. I learned a lot, including how to behave between scenes."

Jeff Townes was thrilled for his recording partner's big-screen success. He joked at the time, "When I saw him in *Made in America* I was shocked. I've never seen Will so big before. He was about twelve feet tall!"

In 1993 Jazzy Jeff & the Fresh Prince released their fifth and final full album together, *Code Red*. Although it was still very definitely a rap album, the music contained on it is far more progressive sounding and more adult than their earlier efforts. Several critics found it to be the strongest and most constantly pleasing album of their recording career.

Explaining their individual roles within the framework of their Grammy-winning duo, Will explained, "I make all the final decisions on the lyrics and Jeff makes all the final decisions on the music."

At that time, Will claimed of 1993's *Code Red*, "This one is definitely the most eclectic piece we've ever done. We generally do slow-tempo, groove-oriented records, but we've got a lot of party-hyper energy on this one. It's about friendship and love."

According to Jeff, "It's got a funky beat you can bug out to. It's pretty hard-hittin' heavy."

With regard to their very different personalities, Will humorously pointed out, "I tend to be more logical. I think I give the most solid advice. Like, there was a time when Jeff didn't want to fly. But he's got to fly to the show because it's too far to drive, right? So I give him good, solid advice: 'Get on the plane and shut up!'

Somehow, from out of the depths of depression, Will was about to experience a huge windfall of good luck.

See, that's logical." On a more serious note Will explained, "Jeff is a feeling man. I let my mind lead me; Jeff lets his heart lead him."

Where his head was leading him at the time was toward a full-fledged career on the big screen. His first two feature-film appearances had given him the experience in front of the movie cameras, and had left him longing for more. He claimed during this era, "I'm still working on my acting skills. I feel I've improved, but I'm still not ready to step out with my own feature." The next film that he appeared in, however, was going to be remembered as his most challenging role to date.

Will in *Made in America*.

Will Smith Facts

Full Name:	Willard Smith II
Nicknames:	"Prince," "The Fresh Prince," "Big Willie," "The Big Williest"
Birthdate:	September 25, 1968
Hometown:	Philadelphia, Pennsylvania
Parents:	Willard Smith, Sr., Caroline Smith
Father's Occupation:	Engineer, formerly the owner of a refrigeration company
Mother's Occupation:	Local School Board
Siblings:	Pam Smith, Harry and Ellen Smith (twins)
Wife:	Jada Pinkett
Ex-Wife:	Sheree Zampino
Children:	Willard Smith III, known as Trey; Jaden Christopher Syre Smith
Singing Partner:	Jeff A. Townes a/k/a Jazzy Jeff and D.J. Jazzy Jeff
Height:	Six feet, two inches
Pets:	Four Rotweilers: Tyson, Gracie, Zachy, Indo
Dream Movie:	Role: Muhammad Ali
If a "Will Smith Special" were on a restaurant menu it would be:	"A big, thick, double fudge brownie with vanilla ice cream, whipped cream, nuts, and a cherry."

Six Degrees of Separation

The Broadway play *Six Degrees of Separation* was known as a totally bizarre one. In fact, it was so strange that it couldn't have been made up out of someone's imagination, it was taken from the only thing stranger than fiction: reality. It is the story of a young black man who decides to scam his way through affluent New York City by impersonating the son of a celebrity, and to play off of people's generosity, guilt, and fears.

Donald Sutherland, Stockard Channing, and Will Smith in *Six Degrees of Separation*.

Pretending to be a character he calls "Paul Poitier," the son of famed actor Sidney Poitier, he is convincingly smooth and suave. In the plot of this real-life scam, he ingratiated his way into the homes of several well-to-do families. He was also gay. Not only was he impersonating the son of a celebrity, he was in actuality impersonating someone who did not exist—because in fact—Sidney Poitier has no son.

In the award-winning John Guare play *Six Degrees of Separation*, there are several semi-explicit gay scenes. When Will Smith auditioned for the role, he himself proclaimed, "If you lined up one hundred films, this would be the last one that people would expect me to do." How true that was. However, that was exactly what he needed to get casting directors' attention in Hollywood.

Potentially acting opposite Donald Sutherland and Stockard Channing if he actually landed this role, he knew that it would be a real feather in his cap. As he explained it, "If I don't do a good job, it's a risk. This isn't a movie you'll take your kids to see. The biggest consideration for me was, if I pull this role off, I'm a legitimate actor. Hollywood doesn't really respect TV actors; film is

As Paul Poitier in *Six Degrees of Separation*.

Six Degrees of Separation put Will on the A-list of young actors in Hollywood.

the medium to succeed in. I want people to know there is something beyond what I can do in *Fresh Prince*. I want to be able to be accepted in any type of endeavor I choose."

He knew what a challenge this would truly be. He also knew that if he didn't do a convincing job on the screen, it could be disastrous. On the other hand, he also knew that he could be sacri-

ficing his rap singing credibility by playing such an uncharacteristic role. "*Six Degrees* was the scariest choice I've ever had to make in my career," he admits. "My big concern was for my rap career—you don't see too many rappers playing homosexual roles in films. The origins of the music are about masculinity, how tough you can be. So I was concerned about how my credibility would be affected."

Yet, the stakes were incredibly huge for him. As he put it, "If I pull off something this dramatic, then Spike Lee and Steven Speilberg will want to work with me."

According to *Six Degrees of Separation* director and screenwriter Fred Schepisi, he was blown away by Smith the first time he read for the part. "Will showed up for our meeting in a three-piece suit and did a number on me, as they say," claims Schepisi. "He did this with such incredible confidence and charm that the very act of his trying to convince me of his abilities did exactly that. He tried to convince me that he'd do whatever it would take, would go through whatever process, was sure he could get himself prepared. That confidence and charm was everything the character should be. He was worth taking a chance on."

Schepisi also knew from the start that Smith's movie experience was limited, and that he was not a trained actor. "Will has the reputation and a name, but this was a work of more substance. We weren't expecting to teach him about the whole acting experience, but we wanted him to have a healthy respect for what's involved," Fred explained.

Will really threw himself into this role. He knew that it was a make-it-or-break-it type of situation. He hired a dialect coach so that he could confidently fit into the role of Paul. The first time he saw the six-page monologue that was to be part of his first scene, he instantly wondered what the hell he had gotten himself into.

With regard to the monologue,

Will laughs, "It almost made me not want to take the role."

When he landed the part, he was thrilled with every aspect of the role—except for one thing. In the stageplay, and in the screenplay of *Six Degrees of Separation*, the character of Paul picks up another young man, and kisses the man on the mouth. When it came time to shoot that scene, Will refused to do the kiss.

"All of that other stuff is acting," Will argued. "But if I kissed him, I kissed him for real." He simply refused to do it. Watching the film, the scene comes up, and due to clever camera angles that catch the back of a head, you can surmise that the two men are obviously kissing, but you never

see a lip-to-lip kiss itself.

"I was wrong," he now admits of his refusal to actually kiss the other actor. "I was definitely wrong. What that is—and now it's more clear to me—is that black people hold their heroes a little more personally responsible for the roles that they choose, because there are so few of us, and black fans can't afford to see us in in compromising roles."

Around this same time in Will's life, he had married Sheree Zampino, and she had given birth to their son, Willard Smith III, whom they call Trey. According to Smith, part of his decision not to perform the kiss in *Six Degrees of Separation* was because of his son.

Will played a smooth con man who worked his way into the homes of affluent New Yorkers.

He explains, "The thing that was a problem for me was my son. I had gotten myself to a 'yes' on all other fronts. That was the only factor I couldn't shake. I was imagining what I would have said to a second grader whose father I just saw kiss a man."

In retrospect he has stated, "It was very immature on my part. I was thinking, 'How are my friends in Philly going to think about this?' I wasn't emotionally stable enough to artistically commit to that aspect of the film. In a movie with actors and a director of this caliber, for you to be the one bringing something cheesy to it, is disappointing. That was a valuable lesson for me. Either you do it or you don't."

When the movie was released, it drew unanimously strong reviews. *Time* magazine claimed, "As Paul, Will Smith is needy, daring, insinuating." *People* found him "remarkable," and *Entertainment Weekly* said that his portrayal in *Six Degrees of Separation* was "an impressive performance."

In choosing to do the role of Paul, Will had hoped that he would get noticed by other directors in Hollywood. Among them was Barry Sonnenfeld, who would

As Paul, Will finds himself embroiled in a web of deception.

eventually direct Will in *Men in Black*. He claimed in 1997 that Will is definitely Academy Award–winning actor just waiting to happen. "I actually think he should have been nominated [for an Oscar] for *Six Degrees*," says Sonnenfeld. "I think he'll have no trouble doing it—probably within the next two or three years."

After he was finished filming *Six Degrees*, he had to return to the next season of *The Fresh Prince of Bel Air*. After speaking proper prep school English for several weeks on the film, he was out of step with the speech patterns of his television character. According to him, "I had to watch all the old episodes and go back to my old neighborhood in Philadelphia and hang with my buddies to get back into the mind-set. To think: I was even starting to like [Paul Poitier's] khaki pants!"

Now that he was becoming an accomplished actor in Hollywood on the big screen, he felt himself growing in self-confidence and on-screen style. It began to trickle down to his regular job as the star of a network television show.

"The fact that I couldn't act was what made *Fresh Prince* popular," he said after filming *Six Degrees of Separation*. "It was so real. People could connect with it.

"If I pull off something this dramatic, then Spike Lee and Steven Speilberg will want to work with me."

When I started the show, I was pretty much just playing myself, but now my life experience has gone beyond the life experience of the character. I'm finding myself having to act more now."

This growth experience was very good for Will. With three films under his belt, he was growing in stature. He was a beloved character in America's living rooms each week due to his television series. Now he was finally ready to make the leap into not only appearing in big Hollywood films, but to starring in them.

Will with Heather Graham and Eric Thal in *Six Degrees of Separation*.

Bad Boys

Will in the last episode of *The Fresh Prince of Bel Air*.

A fter completing the film *Six Degrees of Separation*—which has a very intense, very tightly written screenplay, with very pithy and relevant social commentary about race relations and interpersonal relationships as well—suddenly *The Fresh Prince of Bel Air* was seeming very irrelevant in comparison. The show didn't seem as meaningful or sharp to Will. Almost instantly he wanted to make some changes to update the network situation comedy.

"I sense a great responsibility to make the show cutting edge," Will stated at the time, "and I will no longer tolerate those things I disagree with. I really hate dumb jokes. I'm always fighting it. I keep saying, 'Why can't we be more like *Roseanne*?' That's the best show on TV. I'd love our jokes to have

Martin Lawrence and Will Smith accepting Showest Awards in Las Vegas for their performances in *Bad Boys*.

meaning beyond the superficial humor."

With regard to the light "family-oriented" fare that the scripts of *Fresh Prince* were addressing at the time, Smith explained, "We're talking about a seventeen-year-old black man from the inner city and there are certain things he should be concerned with—sex and drugs, for two. He should have more involvement with friends from the inner city. There will be lots of touchy issues on the show, like prejudice. I want everyone to be enlightened when they watch

our show. We've going to show Americans themselves!"

Needless to say, the producers and writers on the set on *The Fresh Prince of Bel Air* were less than excited about one of the actors telling them what they should be doing. "In Hollywood there's a great resistance to change. I'm being met with much opposition," said Will.

When Will ran into Bill Cosby at a business-oriented function around this same time, he began to complain to Cosby that *The Fresh Prince of Bel Air* didn't have the

snappy kind of writing that he wanted the show to have. According to Will, "When I complained about the writing on the show, Bill suggested I write a script. 'Just write one and don't go to sleep until it's finished,' he told me." So he took Cosby's advice, and took a stab at it. "When I met with the writers the next day," he recalls, "I had a lot less anger and a lot more understanding of the process."

However, he still wasn't happy, so he complained at length to Benny Medina, who in turn complained to the producers of the show, Susan and Andy Borowitz, and a huge clash began. To "cut to the chase," the Borowitzes quit, and a new producer, Winifred Hervy-Stallworth took their place. The fall 1992–1993 season of *The Fresh Prince of Bel Air* became the strongest one yet for the show, and Will was more content with making the series more poignant, and in touch with reality.

His favorite episode from that season was the Christmas show. Instead of non-stop holiday frivolity, the show's fictional family is robbed at gunpoint, and the thieves steal all of the unopened presents. "The point of this episode is that there aren't any monetary gifts. They've all been

stolen. The gifts have been removed, but the heart and the thought that originally went into the gifts is still there," Will explained.

In addition to Will's state of discontent over the weekly scripts, there were also other conflicts on the set of *Fresh Prince*. Viewers were shocked when actress Janet Hubert-Whitten was suddenly fired from the show in 1993.

When the story hit the press, Janet Hubert-Whitten was not hesitant to point her finger toward the reason she was suddenly given her pink slip. "Anyone who stands up to Mr. Smith on *Fresh Prince* is gone," she claimed. "Yes, I reprimanded him constantly for being rude to people and locking himself in his room, but I did not slander him in any way."

When Ms. Hubert-Whitten's statements were published, Will's initial rebuttal was less than complimentary. "I can say straight up that Janet wanted the show to be *The Aunt Viv of Bel Air Show*," he claimed. "She's been mad at me all along. She said once, 'I've been in this business for ten years and this snotty-nosed punk comes along and gets a show.' No matter what, to her I'm just an Antichrist."

For whatever reason, Will was compelled to issue a much tamer statement, which read, "Janet Hubert-Whitten was an incredible actress. She brought so much spirit and fun and warmth to *Fresh Prince*. She made that set a home. She was really special. Of course, there was pain in her leaving, but she thought it was me, which kind of irritated me, but people make their own beds and have to sleep in them. I didn't have anything to do with it. She just never believed that." Whatever the reasoning, what were they going to do about the part of Aunt Viv? It was decided that the character would still be a pivotal part of the plot of the show, but that the actress would simply change.

Daphne Maxwell Reid, who had previously been seen in the TV series *Frank's Place*, came in and took over the role of Aunt Viv. According to her at the time, "I was afraid of being known as

Will Smith and Karyn Parsons in *The Fresh Prince of Bel Air*.

the 'replacement.' I thought there would be strain, like my being a stepmother."

However, she was thrilled to find just the opposite. "These people opened their arms and their hearts. It was like they wanted me there and treated me so well. I came in fresh and uninformed. Now it feels like I've been a part of that family all along. We just have a ball," she stated at the time.

The only acknowledgment that came out in the plot of the show was a line which Jazzy Jeff delivered. In Daphne's first scene on the series, Jeff turned to her and said, "You sure have changed since you had that baby." After that, the atmosphere on the set truly was that of one big happy family.

Even Will and Tatyana Ali were getting along at this point in the show. Their relationship had been a bit frosty the first season. Will had thought of Tatyana as just a cute little girl, and he had talked down to her. She had felt that he was nothing more than a famous wannabe actor. However, in the three seasons that they had worked together, they became

One of Will's favorite *Fresh Prince* episodes was the Christmas one, where the family had to look within to find the true meaning of the holiday.

Will in the final episode of *The Fresh Prince of Bel Air.*

friends. Tatyana was also reaching the age when teenage girls look at older boys in a different light than they did before. Ali remembers arriving on the set of the show one day, and Will was wearing an especially sexy pair of leather pants. According to her, "I turned to someone and said, 'Gosh, Will has a really cute butt!'" Suddenly, working with him wasn't such a chore anymore.

Meanwhile, Will had other things on his mind. He was quite serious about getting more involved in his work on feature films. When casting was underway for an actor to portray the role of Robin in *Batman Forever,* Will seriously wanted to land that role. Unfortunately for him, the role went to Chris O'Donnell.

However, what he did end up with was a cop buddy film with Martin Lawrence, called *Bad Boys.* Similar in character to the roles Nick Nolte and Eddie Murphy played in *48 Hours,* and Mel Gibson and Danny Glover have portrayed in the *Lethal Weapon* series of films, *Bad Boys* seemed like the perfect film for Will to star in.

When producer Jerry Bruckheimer first suggested Will Smith as one of the leads for *Bad Boys,* he claims that the Hollywood brass was less than impressed with that suggestion. Now that Will has become big news in Hollywood via *Independence Day* and *Men in Black,* of course, everyone sees Bruckheimer's foresight. Says Jerry, "They had offers to every other actor; but no one was available. When I said I wanted Will, they looked at me like *I* was an *alien.*"

At that very same time, another film was being cast, which Will had desired to land more. According to him, "Something I wanted real bad but didn't get was Blair Underwood's role in *Just Cause* with Sean Connery. It was shooting in Miami the same time we were doing *Bad Boys.* The producers and director said, 'We'll take a meeting, but we already know it's "no." The role's too close to what you did in *Six Degrees of Separation.*'" With that, he dove right into his work on *Bad Boys,* with a great deal of enthusiasm. What he wanted to accomplish with this role was to prove once and for all to Hollywood that he was capable of carrying a film himself, as one of its two main stars.

"My role in *Bad Boys* is completely different from anything I have ever done," Will explained. "He [the character of Mike Lowrey] is a playboy and I have never been a playboy. On screen and in real life, I've always been the guy who couldn't get the girl. I like the change and I like the stretch. I went from *Fresh Prince* to *Six Degrees* and back to *Fresh Prince* and now to *Bad Boys*. I enjoy doing different things and trying to keep the audience off balance. I really like that a lot."

Will essentially plays himself, a meticulous bon vivant, who is also a playboy. As Mike Lowrey, he is extra fussy about his appearance and his possessions. In the opening sequence, when Martin Lawrence drops greasy French fries on the pristine carpeting of his $100,000+ sports car, Will nearly has a coronary attack.

The film presented a nice juxtapositioning for the two actors. While Will portrays the role of the playboy, notorious womanizer Martin is cast as the settled-down family man with kids.

In the plot of the film, someone has stolen a huge stack of confiscated heroin from a Miami police station, and there is a strong possibility that it is an

"inside job." Actress Téa Leone is the roommate of a high-class call girl. Accompanying her to a paid drug party turns into a lush Floridian nightmare when she witnesses a double murder.

What unfolds from there is a flamboyant shoot-'em-up with lots of violence and lots of bullets and blood. Through a strange twist in circumstances, Smith and Lawrence are mistaken for each other, and they have to switch roles. Now Smith must play housefather, and Lawrence has to fend off women's advances. Feisty Téa decides to take matters into her own hands, and shows up at a discotheque to avenge the murder of her friend, and gets involved in an explosive causeway chase scene. Just to complete the *Miami Vice*/Caribbean flavor of the film, while the final credits roll, they do so to an upbeat reggae version of the song "Bad Boys" by singing stars Inner Circle.

While filming *Bad Boys*, Will reportedly had a blast in Miami. According to him, "As much as it is a movie, it's real too. There's a

He was beginning to feel like he was spinning his wheels working on network television.

lot of physical work that goes into it."

In addition, the movie's two stars hit it off instantly. According to Martin Lawrence, "When I met Will, there was an immediate chemistry on camera, we'd be cool. We opened our hearts to each other and decided, yeah, we could be partners."

Will echoed those feelings by stating, "I think the key to a good partnership is developing that mental link where you can just look at someone and know what's up. It's Will and Martin, but it's a real action movie with some really good action sequences. Working with Martin was great. He's a comedic genius; in fact, he's a comedic geyser. We'd never worked together before, but it never felt like we were strangers— we got to really know each other. The chemistry was really great."

When the reviews of *Bad Boys* came out, it was unanimous, Will Smith had a hit on his hands. *Rolling Stone* magazine proclaimed, "The climatic shootout inside an airplane hangar, complete with a 727 blowing sky high, slides the film into overdrive. It's all special-effects noise and nonsense. We're not fooled. Lawrence and Smith are the real firecrackers. . . . The unfailingly ingratiating Smith glides through the movie. . . . Smith is an actor with a refined sense of comedy. He is also physically imposing enough to pull off a serious action film."

Entertainment Weekly was equally as glowing: "There's a spark of canniness in casting Lawrence and Smith against type. Smith, the clean-cut sitcom prince,

plays the swinging bachelor, and Lawrence, notorious for the raunchiness of his stand-up routines, is the devoted family man. . . . Lawrence and Smith are winningly smooth comic actors. Smith especially holds the camera with his matinee-idol sexiness and his quicksilver delivery of lines."

Bad Boys did very well at the box-office when it was released in 1995. It grossed $140 million in the United States, and an additional $75 million globally.

When Will returned to Hollywood to film the 1995–1996 sea-

son of *The Fresh Prince of Bel Air*, he again had problems with the show's relevancy. Two years before, Will had started making motions like the television show had perhaps accomplished all that it could accomplish. "Artistically," he pondered, "the show has made me feel somewhat crazed, but I'll stick with it through the end of my contract."

He was beginning to feel like he was spinning his wheels working on network television. "When I got into this business, the most important thing for me was to

Will and the cast in the 149th and last episode of his TV show.

Clowning around with the cast and crew at the wrap party that followed.

always try to stay on the edge. It's really difficult with television to be anywhere near the edge, especially Monday night at 8:00 P.M.," he claimed. "I felt like it was time to end the show. We had a nice run. I had done movies like *Six Degrees of Separation* and *Bad Boys*, I was up for more—including *Independence Day*—and the TV show just felt confining. You're pretty much one character [on television], and there are not many peaks and valleys, just pretty much the same old, same old. And I wanted to go

out while we were still good. You get up to eight or nine seasons and then you're struggling. I wanted to go out solid while we were still funny."

The reality was that he had outgrown the series. According to him, "It became increasingly difficult to find that guy inside me. All the things Fresh Prince stood for, all the fun he had, still exist inside me, it's just that those aren't the dominant aspects of my personality anymore."

One of the last episodes of the

TV series was among Will's absolute favorites. On the episode, the father who deserted his fictional character reappeared, and was portrayed by actor Ben Vereen. According to Will, "I thought it was very important to see something in the character who plays Will's father—to be able to see where Will got his charisma from. But there had to be another element as well. The father, after all, had deserted Will—the old man had to have a special quality so the audience wouldn't hate him.

I thought that he really needed to be a character who was someone you could listen to . . . before you passed judgment. Ben Vereen is one of the only actors in Hollywood who could've made that character believable."

It wasn't with any sense of regret that he completed the program's final season. He just wanted to make certain that the show went off the air while it was still fresh and exciting. He was also proud of the work he had done for the six seasons it had been on the air. "From the fan mail I've received, I know the show helped many teens get through difficult situations in their lives. We've touched on real problems kids have—drug use, sex, prejudices, inner-city problems. Even if we couldn't offer them solutions, our show has shown them that they are not alone," Will said sincerely.

In the plot of the last episode of *The Fresh Prince of Bel Air*, the cast was making plans to split up. After the characters of Ashley and Hilary decided to move to New York City, Aunt Vivian and Uncle Phil, Nickey and Carlton decided to join them on the East Coast. Even the butler, Geoffrey, was going back to his native England. And the character of Will was opting to remain in Los Angeles, where he was planning on attending college.

It was an episode filled with joy and laughter, and some tender moments as well. The character of Uncle Phil turned to Will and said in a misty-eyed fashion, "I remember a kid loaded with all the potential in the world, and now I see a person on the verge of realizing that potential."

Not only was that statement apropos for the fictional character of Will on the TV show, but it was also prophetically about the real-life actor Will Smith, as he was about to enter a new phase in his show business career.

There was a huge "wrap" party after the cameras stopped turning on that final episode. In the six years an impressive 149 episodes had been filmed. Recalled Tatyana, "I think I spent ten or fifteen minutes crying my eyes out, like everybody else in the cast, because it was all over."

As the show came to its conclusion, Will publicly stated, "Everyone on this show is the best. The writers, producers, directors—the greatest cast in television. I respect them all."

He felt happy with what the show had accomplished, and for all that he had learned during the show's long and successful run. According to him, "The audience related the character to reality. When I said a line, the audience didn't feel I was acting. What that allowed me as an artist was to more effectively carry my audience wherever I wanted them to go."

It was around this same time that Will's first marriage, to Sheree Zampino, crumbled. When Sheree announced to him that she wanted a divorce, he was devastated. In time, however, he grew to respect her decision to pull the plug on their union. What most upset him was that his son, Trey, was having to deal with the divorce at such a young age. "It's

"Everyone on this show is the best. The writers, producers, directors—the greatest cast in television. I respect them all."

It wasn't long before the party turned into a riotous food fight.

not the perfect situation," Will said with resolve, "but that's what life has dealt. We all make mistakes, and we have to find the good thing out of it. What was a mistake for me created the most beautiful thing I've ever seen in my life," he says, referring to Trey.

"I had no business getting married. Neither one of us was ready. We hadn't experienced enough life yet to be together."

Like the old saying goes, "When one door closes, another one opens." In Will Smith's life this was exactly the case.

Although *The Fresh Prince of Bel Air* was ending, and his first marriage was ending, he was on the threshold of a wonderful new phase in his life.

Independence Day

Looking back on his divorce, in time Will was able to honestly say, "Actually, I think [Sheree] did me a favor. But I'm hugely family oriented. To me, a child being able to hear thunder outside and to run and jump into bed with his mother and father—I remember that from Philly. That's a memory my son will never have. For me, I can't imagine life being any better than it is for me. . . . But there's still a pain that I feel, that my son will never experience some of the beauty that I experienced of having a family. There's almost a kind of weird guilt from my extreme happiness."

The "extreme happiness" that Will speaks of has to do with his personal life, which has been made both exciting and fulfilling, due to the arrival in his life of Jada Pinkett. Jada and

Will Smith and Jeff Goldblum prepare to save the world in *Independence Day*.

Will dragging an alien across the desert in *Independence Day*.

Will senses that there is something wrong in his neighborhood in *Independence Day*.

Will had originally met on the set of *The Fresh Prince of Bel Air*, when she came to audition for the role of one of his love interests on the program. However, at the time, the producers of the show felt that, at the height of five feet tall, she was too petite to be believable on camera with six-foot-two Will.

Since that early 1990s audition, Jada and Will remained friends. Meanwhile, Jada has amassed quite an impressive resume of film and television roles. Her big break in Hollywood came with a regular role in the comedy series *A Different World*. To date, her film credits include *Menace II Society*, *Jason's Lyric*, *The Nutty Professor*, *Set It Off*, *Scream 2*, and *A Low Down Dirty Shame*.

Jada is pretty, cute, sultry, charming, and outspoken. In other words, she was just what Will needed in his life at that time. According to her, she was born with self-confidence and a sense of determination: "I was a star before I was a star. When I was growing up, Baltimore was mine—I owned it. Everybody knew me. I was always putting on productions. I was everywhere—parties, skating rinks, any crowd, any club. From punk rockers to homeboys, I was in every circle."

Like Will, Jada came from a family that put a great value on education. She explains, "My grandmother was adamant about having well-rounded, well-edu-cated people in her family. She always made it very clear that there was nothing I could not do. I grew up believing that. And when you have that type of determination, nobody can stop you." This gave Jada and Will a lot in common from the very start.

Explaining her relationship with Smith at that time, Jada says, "We were friends first, and then the love thing came around second, and that's how it still is. When he was going through his difficulties in his marriage and I had just broken up with Grant Hill, the basketball player—I like big men—we just kind of came together. It took me by surprise. To me, Will just used to be a goofy, lanky, plays-too-much guy. He used to get on my nerves. Then we went to dinner one night and I saw something totally different in him. He was stressed about his marriage and he was talking about all these different things, and I was, like, 'He's a man now. He's got a kid. He's been married. He's actually grown up.' It kind of grew from there, slowly but surely."

When they reconnected, Jada found Will to be very unhappy about his break-up with Sheree. "Will was distraught and needed a place to release," Jada claims. "He was talking about how he would sleep in the car outside the house to make sure [Trey and Sheree] were okay. I thought that was incredible. I'd never seen that side of Will before. It's not a side he wears on his sleeve. And then one thing just led to another."

Will recalls, "Jada was like part of our small Hollywood community, everyone kind of knows one another. When . . . I got divorced, Jada was there to take care of me."

He also laughs, "She claims she was never attracted to me. Now she's all in love with me and that nurturing mother side came out."

She was in his life when the most important film of his career came along. It was called *Independence Day*, and it was destined to place Will Smith on the A-list of Hollywood leading men. An elaborate science fiction film about Earth battling creatures from another planet, it was the most anticipated film of 1996, and was the biggest hit of the year.

When Will was awarded the role in *Independence Day*, he instantly began screening every disaster film he could get his hands on. He wanted to make certain that his performance had the right balance of seriousness, with just a touch of tongue-in-cheek humor to

balance it. The film he paid the closest amount of attention to was the shipwreck epic *Poseidon Adventure*. The actor he most closely observed and identified with was that of Ernest Borgnine. According to Will, "I watched Borgnine's performance about 20 times before *Independence Day*. Because he was funny in a life-and-death situation. But he wasn't funny ha-ha, he was deadly serious. What I learned from Borgnine is you can stand there straight and just say a line, and let the moment make it funny."

When he showed up on the

set of the film, Will instantly bowled over everyone he came in contact with. Dean Devlin, who produced and co-wrote *Independence Day* proclaimed that anything Smith wanted to accomplish, he was surely capable of attaining. "Just watch him in *Six Degrees of Separation*," said Devlin. "If this guy wanted to be president, get ready!"

Playing the part of a fighter pilot who sets out to "kick E.T.'s ass," Will was also a huge hit with the cast as well. According to actress Vivica A. Fox, who played the part of his wife in *Indepen-*

This kiss won the MTV Movie Award as the year's best screen make-out scene.

73

Will was obsessed with carving a name for himself as a movie star.

dence Day, "My favorite part of his face is his lips. They're full and luscious, and when he smiles, they're warm and inviting." Was it any wonder that the MTV Movie Award for the year's best on-screen kiss went to Vivica and Will for *Independence Day*?!

As an adventure film, *Independence Day* is a huge ensemble piece. While the most impressively staged sequences involved pyrotechnics and special effects, there are several human stories intertwined throughout the plot. The cast also included Harry Con-

nick Jr., Jeff Goldblum, Judd Hirsch, Randy Quaid, Robert Loggia, Harvey Fierstein, Adam Baldwin, Bill Pullman as the President of the United States, and Mary McDonnell as his First Lady.

According to Will Smith, "I loved Bill Pullman's performance, but I got the great lines and situations. Maybe a lot of it has to do with television training, though. Watch Jim Carrey, Tom Hanks, Robin Williams, or Eddie Murphy, who all come from comedy television where you learn to maximize every one hundredth of a

second. These guys know that when you do a half hour of television, probably nine minutes of it are yours and that's it. From the first season of *Fresh Prince* on, I got [a copy of] every TV show and every movie [Carrey, Hanks, Williams, and Murphy] made, and I watched them over and over to see the differences between the two mediums. I saw that—outside of Jim Carrey—everything in movies is just a touch smaller, a touch slower, because the camera does more of the work in a film. I sat down, and still do, with an incredible management team to discuss the theory of a TV star versus a movie star, the concept of celebrity versus stardom versus a real actor. I knew I was going to want to make the transition to movies, so I started off really small—just to get the feel of a movie set and the film world— with *Where the Day Takes You*."

Now that he had been a successful rap singer, the star of his own hit television series, and a film actor, he wanted to make certain that he excelled at every single project he became involved in. Will was obsessed with carving out a name for himself as a movie star. He is so serious about his aspirations that he studies the films of his competition and takes note of

Will and Harry Connick Jr. prepare to "kick E.T.'s ass."

their individual career moves.

"Now, I want to be in that place that Robin Williams is—say, where they'll offer him roles that are similar to Mork from Ork, but they'll also offer him *Mrs. Doubtfire* and *Awakenings*. Right now, I'm watching a lot of Nicholas Cage, because he's in that place, too. He can do *Raising Arizona* and *Leaving Las Vegas*. I'm also studying everything Cary Grant ever did. I want to position myself in a place where people will offer me anything," he claims.

Independence Day was an instant smash when it was released in 1996. It raked in a record $100 million plus at the box-office the first week it opened. After all of the intergalactic dust cleared, it had become the hugest-grossing film of the year, taking in more than $300 million.

No one was more excited about the success of the film than Will's own father. According to Will, "The Monday the first box-office numbers were announced, he woke me up by calling me from Philly at nine A.M., which made it six A.M. in L.A. He'd just seen the numbers and said, 'Boy, you remember when I told you that if you work hard and focus you can have anything you want?' I said, 'Yeah, Dad, I remember,' and then

Independence Day made Will Smith a box-office hero in 1996.

he said, 'That's bull****, boy. You're the luckiest nig*** I ever met in my life.'"

Of all the audience members who saw Will on the screen in *Independence Day* and got excited about what they saw, Jada Pinkett was truly his Number One Fan. Speaking of the scene where Smith has to drag a dead alien across the desert, Pinket gleefully claimed of his rippling muscles, "He was ripped! I was like, 'I can't wait to get the laser disc!' When Will and I want to have a romantic night, before he comes home I always watch the scene in *Bad Boys* when his shirt is hanging open and he's running down the street in slow-mo [slow motion]. He'll call me on the phone and be like, 'I'm on my way home,' and I'll be like,

'Well, you know what to expect because I just watched that scene in *Bad Boys*. I'm going to be nice and ready when you get here."

Only seven years ago, Will was at the most depressed phase of his life. Having blown all of his rap recording money, and staring bankruptcy seriously in the face, he had rebuilt his life thanks to *The Fresh Prince of Bel Air*. Now that the television show was over, and he was really relying on the success of his movie acting career to support him, *Independence Day* was truly the litmus paper of "success" or "failure." The world that he had saved on the big screen in *Independence Day* was the same one on which he was now sitting firmly atop.

Men in Black

Will Smith packed some more summer movie power in *Men in Black*.

While *Independence Day* suddenly made Will Smith *the* leading man to watch for in Hollywood, the problem now became one of finding the right vehicle to follow it up with. Thankfully, with *Men in Black*, he not only matched the intensity and success of *Independence Day*, in many aspects of the project, he surpassed it!

According to Will, it was *Independence Day* that was directly responsible for landing him *Men in Black*. "It's certainly put me on the map as far as my career's concerned," reveals Smith. "Steven Spielberg called me afterwards and told me about his new movie. He didn't ask me if I wanted to do it, he just said, 'You have to do this movie.' You can't really turn him down can you?" No, obviously he could not, and it was a good thing he didn't.

When the film was released in the summer of 1997, it became the coolest, the hottest, and the baddest hit to grace the big screen. Describing his role in the movie,

A routine trip to a pawn shop launches Will on an alien adventure.

Will explained, "I play a New York cop who joins a government agency to monitor alien activity on Earth. Me and Tommy Lee Jones get caught up in the middle of an intergalactic terrorist plot and we have to stop the world being destroyed."

The first time we see Will Smith in *Men in Black*, he is chasing a criminal on the streets of Manhattan. He is a plainclothes policeman, chasing a street punk. However, it turns out not to be just any punk. The criminal is a superhuman alien from another planet, who scales the Guggenheim Museum's outer wall with the ability of an insect.

After Tommy Lee Jones and Smith pay a bizarre visit to a pawn shop accused of selling "hot" intergalactic weapons, an uneasy friendship is struck upon. After watching Smith's performance at the pawn shop, Tommy Lee invites Will to an audition/interview to be part of a mysterious organization identified only as MIB.

Tommy Lee explains that Earth is being used as a holding space for aliens from another planet, 1,500 of them, most of them in Manhattan. According to Jones, among the technological developments that Earth has already adapted from alien designs are velcro fastening tape, microwave ovens, and a miniature Life Saver candy-sized disk that will soon replace the compact disk.

In addition, Dionne Warwick, Sylvester Stallone, and a host of other well-known celebrities are all aliens, disguised as humans, and monitored by the organization. Says Smith, "Michael Jackson, Dennis Rodman, and Steven Spielberg and some others are supposedly aliens. It's the Men in Black's job to make sure that they stay in line." When Will Smith, as Agent Jay, officially joins the organization, all traces of his identity are erased, along with fingerprints and Social Security number. He is issued his MIB black suit, and Ray-Ban shades, and voila: he is officially one of the Men in Black.

It seems that one of the dangerous aliens is on the loose. To protect himself Will gets the Noisy Cricket, a tiny little pistol, while Tommy Lee gets a more exotic model. Although Will looks at the Noisy Cricket with disgust, like it is some miserable and lame toy, when he fires it, he soon discovers that it packs such an impact it propels him backward into walls and cars. "Tommy has a big, cool-sounding gun, it's some kind of de-atomizer. He gives me a little gun, the Noisy Cricket. It's only about an inch and a half long, but every time I shoot it, it throws me 20 yards!"

Some of the most dramatic—and outlandish—scenes come at the climax of a battle with a giant insect from outer space. As Will explains it, "Yeah, and that slime is horrible! Tommy Lee Jones blows an alien up, and it splashes all over me. I was completely drenched in alien guts. Ack! It was really disgusting!"

According to director Barry Sonnenfeld, it was the scenes in which the actors were spattered with the blue slime, or methylcel-luloid, that were the most talked about. "Will hated it," Barry explains, "but Tommy didn't mind at all, and I think Tommy didn't mind because Will hated it. He got to be the old hand, the professional. Will, who never whined or complained, was going, 'Oh man, how many more shots?' Tommy was saying to his wardrobe peo-ple, 'More. Pour more on.'"

According to Will, "Tommy Lee is a rancher. He's used to birthing cattle and getting covered in nasty, gooey stuff. I'm from the inner city."

That slime was truly Smith's least favorite part of the filming process. "Listen, that was the most disgusting," he claims. "I

Will interviewing to become a top-secret man in black. Once he landed the job, the red jacket was history.

don't know what was mixed up in there, but it was like some kind of fleshy stuff. It was three 16 hour days of having that goo in my hair, my mouth."

The weapons and the imaginative technology in *Men in Black* were every bit as entertaining as the plot of the film itself. When asked what his favorite gadget was, Will replied, "The neuralizer. With it, I can erase any person's memory, to the second, from any point in their life. I can set the neuralizer for 15 minutes ago, flash it in your face, and it erases the last 15 minutes of your memory. And then I can tell you what your memory is, and that's what you'll remember. That's why Tommy Lee and I need to wear the dark glasses—if we don't have them on, we'll erase our own memories."

One of the most exciting aspects of filming this outrageous movie came with Will's opportunity to bring Trey to see the set of the *Men in Black* headquarters. "I took my son to see it," he recalls, "and he loved this little alien that looked like a tiny scary octopus. He's really nasty looking, and he scoots around on the ground. It's his job to clean the floors!"

When he was asked for tips on spotting aliens walking among us, Will said with a laugh, "It's really difficult to spot one because they could be anything—people or animals. There's a dog in the movie that's an alien. Tommy Lee has to shake him down. Aliens generally excel, though. Michael Jordan is potentially an alien. Tiger Woods is potentially an alien. No human being can win the Masters his first time out and shoot minus 18! Tiger Woods is definitely an alien! . . . In one scene, Sir Perfect of Singhalee wants tickets to a Chicago Bulls game. And I say, 'Oh, don't worry about it, we can do that. Rodman's from that planet.'"

The creatures from other planets were responsible for some of the most exciting cinematic scenes in the film. Academy Award–winning make-up artist and special effects man Rick Baker was responsible for creating the creatures seen in *Men in Black*. According to Baker, "In the *Star Wars* days, it was easy to do something not seen before. But there's been so many sci-fi TV shows and movies since then. With *Men in Black*, I had the freedom to be more comedic with the designs. Realistic but fun. Spielberg was very involved in the design of things. He would say, 'I like the head of this one but not the body.'"

Thanks to the success of *Independence Day*, Will Smith had become one of the most recognized young actors on this—or any other planet. Although it seems like a dream-come-true, it is not without its problems. "I was in Manhattan making *Men in Black*," he explains, "and this girl was driving along, saw me and started mouthing over and over, 'Oh, my God. Oh, my God,' then crashed into another car. Now, she gets out of her car, but she doesn't say, 'Oh, I crashed into the back of a car!' She runs over to me and asks for my autograph. That's when I thought: 'This is real dif-

When Men in Black was released in the summer of 1997, it became the coolest, the hottest, and the baddest hit to grace the big screen.

This pair had some serious weapons for their final showdown with the evil bug from space.

ferent.' Then, I was at the Virgin Megastore in [Times Square in] Manhattan and this girl came up to me, pulled her shirt up and asked me to sign her breasts with a Sharpie. I mean, she's standing there in the middle of the store with her titties hanging out and I'm like, 'Listen, those are really nice breasts, but this is really an inappropriate time and place.' In another store, this toothless 80-year-old lady came up to me, grabbed my face and tried to kiss me right on the lips. I said, 'Now, ma'am, if I walked up to you, grabbed your face and tried to kiss you on the mouth, the cops would give me a Rodney King [beating] and take me right to jail.' And she was like, 'Oh, stop being mean. Just give me a kiss.' I mean, geriatric tongue kisses are pretty much out in my book."

Men in Black's leading lady, Linda Fiorentino, had nothing but wonderful things to say about him. What she remembers most about the film's shoot was that, "Outside Will's trailer were all

Something isn't right in the morgue with Tommy Lee Jones, Will, and Linda Fiorentino.

these eight-year-old kids who watch *Fresh Prince*. He was like the Pied Piper."

Director Barry Sonnenfeld was so thrilled to work with Will that he could hardly wait to prepare another project they could do together. According to Barry, the only other person in Hollywood who is such a delight to work with is Tom Hanks. Comparing Smith to Hanks, Sonnenfeld says, "Both have an incredibly relaxed and real style of performance and they are both incredibly self-confident and normal. Not only are they both performers who came out of TV sitcoms, but both are very confident about who they are. And, of course they are both funny people who are not surrounded by demons."

When the film was released in the summer of 1997, it became an instant hit. Audiences and critics alike absolutely loved it. Giving *Men in Black* four of four stars in its review, *USA Today*'s Susan Wilszczyna called it, "The snappy sci-fi hoot *Men in Black*, a kind of *Independence Day* for smart people, confirms those suspicions and more by expanding on the urban legend that aliens live among us and take on human form . . . Smith's cocky ex-cop soon learns nothing is what it seems as he's shown the intergalactic gooey ropes by Jones' veteran. . . . The out-there premise is irresistible as well as unsettling because, hey, it could be true."

After Smith's whole *Men in Black* adventure came to a close, everyone wanted to know what souvenirs he retained from the film's shoot. "I gave the suit to Planet Hollywood in New York, but I kept a Noisy Cricket, the little gun we used in the movie."

One of the most exciting aspects of the whole *Men in Black* phenomenon was the fact that it brought Will Smith back to the recording studio for the first time since the release of the *Code Red* album. Will had become totally disgusted with what had been happening in the rap music arena, and had no interest in having any part in it. "I'd almost stopped listening to rap," he explains. "Wycleff [Jean] was the person that got me started again. When the Fugees dropped, and then Nas and Jay-Z, I started coming back in. . . . Then, after 'Pac [Tupac Shakur] and Biggie [Smalls] got killed, I felt like, I *have* to make records. Even if I don't have a hit, I'm putting my energy out there, because the vibe of rap was just sh**ty. I was like, 'F*** it, if people don't like my records, fine, but I'm putting 'em out.' I want my son to have a rap record with no profanity—clean and fun."

After the recent shooting deaths of Biggie Smalls and Tupac Shakur, Will began to feel that perhaps it was time for someone to lead the musical genre out of its doldrums. "Rap's gone through a sort of dark ages," he claims. "I think with the loss of Biggie and

Tupac, the rap industry is ready for a change. I'm just feeling good to be part of the renaissance. Rap got away from the essence. The essence of rap was always about partying and having fun. The best rapper was the one that could rock the crowd. How well you shot a gun wasn't part of the criteria."

His views on rap music have remained unchanged throughout the years. According to him, it should still have a sense of "fun" attached to it. "Rap is still young," says Will. "It hasn't completed the circle that other musical genres have completed. The essence was always, 'Good Times'—Chic [the disco group], you know? I believe rap is gonna come back to that simplicity of the beats. I was just listening to an old school tape Jeff made, [and I was thinking] how similar the rap of 10, 15 years ago is to the flavor of what Puffy's doing and that whole Bad Boy [Records] family."

Excited about going into the recording studio again, Will came up with the theme for *Men in Black*, adopting the old Patrice Rushin song "Forget Me Nots" into an exciting and fun rap.

Jada Pinkett, Will Smith, and his son, Trey, and a nephew, at the premiere of *Men in Black*.

With <u>Men in Black</u>, he not only matched the intensity and success of <u>Independence Day</u>, in many aspects of the project, he surpassed it!

However, when he went to his record company, they couldn't have cared less. "[Jive Records] turned down the *Men in Black* song, saying it wasn't a hit. So that fired me up," he claims.

Having given Jive Records the option, he then turned to Columbia Records, who were planning to release the soundtrack album for *Men in Black*. They were thrilled to have Will Smith as part of their roster. He certainly got the last laugh on this deal. He proudly proclaims of the success of the monsterously huge hit single that he scored: "Just for the record, 'Men in Black' was the most-played record in the history of rap."

Jive Records' loss was Columbia's gain. Will's new album was destined to be the biggest one of his entire career. Speaking of the *Big Willie Style* album, Columbia Records executive Samuel Sapp claimed, "He's stepped up the rap on this album. It's kind of an extension of the 'Men in Black'

[single] record. The music has a harder edge, but the lyrics are still very positive—no negative vibes. For example, one song, 'Just the Two of Us,' is about his son, Trey. And, 'Yes, Yes Y'all' is just a fun song—definitely a party record."

One of the most notable things that happened with the release of the *Big Willie Style* album was the fact that he was now using his own name, and he no longer called himself "The Fresh Prince." Thanks to his film career, he can now proclaim, "I'm more known around the world as Will Smith now."

What made the creation of this album such a joy was the fact that Columbia Records rolled the red carpet out for him. "This is the first time I've been able to make a record without any financial constraints," says Smith. "Whatever video I saw in my head; whatever producers I wanted to work with. I had everything at my disposal and this was

my opportunity with no excuses."

Just to keep some continuity going, Jazzy Jeff, Will's long-time musical partner, makes an appearance on two of the cuts on the *Big Willie Style* album, on the songs "Don't Say Nothin'" and "It's All Good." According to Will, "We recorded it in Jeff's house. We're not going in the studio, we're doing this in the crib."

He was also very excited about being back in the recording studio. "Music is the most difficult creative form. Music is like a baby, you gotta nurture it, every second of your life has to be dedicated to the music. It's really a huge undertaking," he says.

So, what's up with this "Big Willie Style" phrase? Explains Will himself, "Being a Big Willie is not about what kind of car you drive, it's not really that. Being a Willie is in your attitude. Being a Willie is based on other things, so-called Willies use different measuring tools than I use. For me, the ultimate Willie tool, the Willie measuring stick, the Willie litmus test, is intellect. I always appreciated Chuck D, Melle Mel, Rakim, and KRS-One for their intellect. There's thought in their rhymes, a lot of times you see people, these so-called Willies not coming up with anything."

Illuminating a bit more on the Big Willie philosophy, Smith claims, "When you say someone is a Willie, it means they're at the top of whatever they do. Michael Jordan is a Big Willie in basketball. Donald Trump is a Big Willie in business. I consider myself a Big Willie in the world of rap. And it kind of works out, because my name is Willie."

In February of 1998, when Will Smith won his third Grammy Award, this time around for "Men in Black," he was able to state with glee, "My previous record company thought that my career was over. Columbia didn't think so."

When asked why there had been such a long absence from singing and songwriting for him, Will replied, "For the past couple years, my life was more emotionally strenuous. It kept me from writing. Now my life is in order. I'm in love and my family is happy." The artist formerly know as "The Fresh Prince" was now maxin' and relaxin' *Big Willie Style*, and enjoying every minute of it.

Jada and Will boogie down at the premiere party for Will's 1997 album, *Big Willie Style*. Sony Records executive Tommy Mottola looks on with a smile.

Big Willie and Jada

Jada and Will at the Blockbuster Awards, 1998.

Aside from his phenomenally successful career, the most exciting thing in Will's life at the moment is the love of his life, Jada Pinkett. They have been next to inseparable ever since she brought him out of his post-divorce blues. According to Smith, "Jada Pinkett is my best friend, and when you can combine your best friend in the world with the person who is also your lover and your partner, that is an emotional and spiritual and physical ecstasy that is unmatched. Basically, she's cool!"

It seems as if, since the minute that they united, they have been running a non-stop mutual admiration society. Will just

The dazzling pair at the Showest Awards in Las Vegas, in 1997.

While Will is methodical, Jada is mercurial. Somehow they balance each other out.

loves her energy, and her supportiveness towards him. "Jada is the first person I've been with who's willing to accept that it's not always going to be great, but that that's okay," Will says.

"He is so precious to me. Not only is he my lover, he is my best friend," Jada says of Smith.

Having just starred in her own 1998 hit film, *Woo*, it is predicted that the next big star in Hollywood just may be Jada. Her biggest fan is obviously Will, who feels she has sheer superstar potential. "I don't need to be a superstar," she claims, however. "Will is always like, 'You could be huge! Worldwide!' And I'm like, 'I don't want it. It's too much.' I'd have to compromise my family. Will understands that."

Together, they make a wonderful team. "Will and I are always in debates. He's my best friend in the whole world, but we're not mirror images. Like, I'm very edgy, and he's commercial. So he's made me a little fluffier, and I've made him a little edgier," she says.

She is also the first to admit they are very different. "Will loves everybody, and everybody loves Will—that's just how he works," Jada states. "But with me, there's some people who love me and some people who hate me. It's never in between. People always know where they stand with me. That makes some people uncomfortable, but I need that kind of clarity in my life."

They had become so close in fact, that everyone was wondering when they were going to just go ahead and get married. But, neither was ready for that commitment. Throughout 1997, during *Men in Black* mania, they kept evading the issue, although they had moved into the same house.

Will simply gave Jada free reign with the decorating of their new love nest. According to her at the time, "We have so many nooks three feet from each other. There's a lot of conversation areas. And everything here is based on communication. That's why we don't have a TV in the

bedroom. That's where we do most of our talking—every night and day. It's like our temple. When my girlfriends come over, we have tea and talk. Life revolves around relationships."

It was late in 1997 that something happened to change their hesitance with walking down the wedding aisle: Jada discovered that she was pregnant.

"At first it was a shock," she claims. "For the first three days it was all these mixed feelings. I was doubting myself, wondering what was going to happen to my career. Then one day I woke up and said to Will, 'You know what? I don't give a f***. I love you. We're going to have a baby.' And then we just got so freaking happy about it."

According to her, Will had his doubts: "Will and I had a very strong conversation about it. I told him, 'You can be unhappy if you want, but we'll be living in the same house—you'll be on one side, and I'll be on the other. It ain't going to be no divorce in here. That's not even an option. So let's talk it all out.' And we talked and talked and talked."

Finally, they decided to just go ahead with it. On December 31, 1997, at a mansion in Baltimore, Maryland, known as the Cloisters,

Will Smith and Jada Pinkett became husband and wife. It wasn't a big showy show business event; it was a closed affair for family and close friends.

As a surprise to her new husband, when she was introduced on stage at January 1998's *Golden Globe Awards* telecast, she insisted her name be announced as "Jada Smith" and not "Jada Pinkett." According to her, her new husband had no idea she was going to do that. "I did it for Will," she says. "It was my cute little introduction to our married life. He didn't know I was doing it. He didn't go to the awards, so he saw it on TV. He loved it; he was very flattered. But on-screen, I'll be Jada Pinkett Smith. No hyphen—to me, the hyphen suggests we can detach anytime we want. But this is glue, Jada Pinkett Smith. Period."

Right on schedule, on July 8, 1998, Jada gave birth to the couple's son. Since Trey's full name was Willard Smith III, the couple named their child Jaden Christopher Syre Smith, using Jada's name as its root.

According to Hollywood insiders, they are as happy as can be. While Will is methodical, Jada is mercurial. Somehow they bal-

Jada and Will at the premiere of
Independence Day, in Hollywood, 1996.

ance each other out. For instance, Will likes to know that everything is in perfect order wherever he goes. He even has to make certain that all of the dollar bills in his pocket are in order, according to value—the larger bills on the outside. According to him, "One, five, 10, 20, 100, and then it's perfect."

Even when he is out shopping with Jada, she has to stand around waiting for him to put the money in the correct order. "I'm ready to go," she says, "he has to do it then and there. But he'll take all his clothes and leave them everywhere."

Naturally, there is talk about Mr. and Mrs. Big Willie Style starring in a film together. They recently came up with a treatment of a screenplay for a feature entitled *Love for Hire*. According to Jada, "We're always creating. We're together '24/7,' so that's not a problem."

Says Will of the project, "I'm developing a romantic comedy. Miss Jada and I would have a ball on camera, but we don't want to mix business with pleasure."

Will is most excited about his 1998 film, *Enemy of the State*. Reportedly, it was a project which was originally offered to Tom

They had others green with envy at the 1997 Academy Awards.

Cruise. In other words, Will has become such a big star that he is definitely on the A-list for the top films being produced today. A thriller, *Enemy of the State* finds Will cast as a man being framed in a governmental cover-up.

Meanwhile, Barry Sonnenfeld, the director of *Men in Black*, has been working on Will's forthcoming big-screen update of *Wild, Wild West*. Sonnenfeld says of Smith, "His self-confidence is so winning that you want to hang out with him and teach you how to be like him."

If Will had to choose between a recording career, or a movie career, which one would he concentrate on? He definitely favors the slower-moving sanity of the film business. "The music industry is the most cut-throat," he claims. "It's strictly 'What can you do for me today?' and 'How much money are you worth to me?' In television, there's a family atmosphere, and on a movie, at least for 16 weeks, it feels more like a family—even though you never see each other again. But with the music industry, ending up broke kind of stabilized me. Your parents tell you that you need to learn the value of a dollar, and you literally have to learn it. Money is really weird and makes people act different. It doesn't change you. Whatever you are and your personality, money magnifies it."

Since his siblings work for him at his production company, Will insists that they are as dedicated about their jobs as he is about his. "I work hard, so I want everyone around me to work hard. If you're not willing to work hard, let someone else do it. It's not really about being tough on writers or directors or anyone else. I'm really tough on lazy people, people who aren't willing to work. I'd rather be with someone who does a horrible job but gives 110 percent than with someone that does a good job and gives 60 percent," he states with conviction.

Speaking of convictions, Will is very definitive about what he believes in, and what he does not. In 1996 when there was a whole controversy about adopting a black English dialect called Ebonics into American school systems, he just about hit the roof. According to plan, spelling and proper English wouldn't be insisted upon for black students in inner-city schools. "I just think that I've worked entirely too hard to learn how to speak English properly for

Having Will's baby! Proudly pregnant new bride Jada, at the Grammy Awards at New York City's Radio City Music Hall, February 1998.

someone to consider Ebonics as a dialect. I just hate it when people make excuses for blacks," he said, blasting the plan.

He is also very definitive when it comes to raising children. According to him, "There's three things that you can give your child. You give them love, you give them knowledge, you give them discipline. You give your kids those three things, and everything else is in the hands of the Lord."

Since he appeared nude in one of the scenes in *Six Degrees of Separation*, he has long been asked if he would ever do a scene with full-frontal nudity. "Men don't have nice fronts," he laughed at the notion. "Penises aren't attractive. Women think they're functional, but not attractive. In fact, the entire male body is not attractive. As naked as I'll ever be is in *Six Degrees of Separation*. Maybe I'll do a love scene, but I'm not showing my balls to nobody. I have a 'no balls' clause. I couldn't just take my balls out anywhere like Harvey Keitel."

According to Will, "What's sexy about being sexy is not trying. Once you become conscious of doing something to be specifically sexy, it's not sexy anymore. I go the other way. Like, when I do a scene, I don't want to do my hair and don't want to put makeup on to specifically try to look sexy. In *Independence Day*, I worked out and wanted my body to look strong, but I was like, 'Nah, let the hair be where it is. Don't put no damn eyeliner on me.'"

Now that Will Smith has become a movie star, and hung up his "Fresh Prince" persona for a while, what has become of Jeff Townes, a/k/a Jazzy Jeff? Actually, he has moved back to the Philadelphia area, where he has his own recording studio. "I had fun [in Los Angeles], but I kept asking myself, 'What am I doing here?' My heart and soul is still music," says Townes. "Will and I know it's because of Jazzy Jeff & the Fresh Prince that I'm able to have the company and he's able to be in *Independence Day*. We respect that. We just move on from there."

Now that Will is back to recording, having scored a huge success with *Big Willie Style*, he will assuredly have to continue. As long as he does, he is certain to get Jazzy Jeff involved. Will has his own recording studio in his house, and he makes music to unwind: "I write the lyrics to rap records as a profession, but I'm not comfortable yet with writing music. So I write music and record it in my studio as a hobby."

What counts most to Will now is his wife, his two sons, and completely throwing himself into whatever projects most interest him. "To me, success is strictly based on how much time you spend doing what you love every day. It's strictly, strictly about passion," he says.

Thanks to his hit films *Independence Day* and *Men in Black*, he will forever be tagged as filmland's most famous defender of the planet Earth. With that kind of an accolade hanging over your head, what new challenges does Will Smith have before him? "I'm going for intergalactic star," he says with a smile. "Why stop at this puny solar system?" Knowing him, that is exactly what he *is* going to do next.

"I want my son to have a rap record with no profanity—clean and fun."

Filmography

Where the Day Takes You
(1992) *
DIRECTOR: Marc Rocco
CAST:
Dermot Mulroney
Robert Knepper
Sean Austin
Balthazar Getty
Will Smith
James Le Gros
Ricki Lake
Lara Flynn Boyle
Peter Dobson
Kyle McLaughlin
Nancy McKeon
Adam Baldwin
Rachel Ticotin
Alyssa Milano
David Arquette
Leo Rossi
Stephen Tobolowsky
Laura San Giacomo
Christian Slater (unbilled)

Made in America *(1993)* *
DIRECTOR: Richard Benjamin
CAST:
Whoopi Goldberg
Ted Danson
Will Smith
Nia Long
Paul Rodriquez
Jennifer Tilly
Peggy Rea
Clyde Kasatsu
Lu Leonard
Frances Bergen
Phyllis Avery

Six Degrees of Separation
(1993) *
DIRECTOR: Fred Schepisi
CAST:
Stockard Channing
Will Smith
Donald Sutherland
Ian McKellen
Mary Beth Hurt
Bruce Davison
Richard Massur
Anthony Michael Hall

Will Smith as TV's Fresh Prince.

Heather Graham
Eric Thai
Anthony Rapp
Osgood Perkins
Catherine Kellner
Jeffrey Abrams
Kitty Carlisle Hart

Bad Boys *(1995)* *
DIRECTOR: Michael Bay
CAST:
Martin Lawrence
Will Smith
Téa Leoni
Theresa Randall
Tchky Karyo
Mary Helgenberger
Anna Thompson

Independence Day *(1996)* *
DIRECTOR: Roland Emmerich
CAST:
Will Smith

Bill Pullman
Jeff Goldblum
Mary McDonnell
Judd Hirsch
Margaret Colin
Randy Quaid
Robert Loggia
James Rebhorn
Harvey Fierstein
Adam Baldwin
Brent Spiner
James Duval
Vivica A. Fox
Lisa Jakub
Ross Bagley
Bill Smitrovich
Harry Connick Jr.

Men in Black *(1997)* *
DIRECTOR: Barry Sonnenfeld
CAST:
Will Smith
Tommy Lee Jones

Rip Torn
Linda Fiorentino
Vincent D'Onofrio

Enemy of the State *(1998)*
DIRECTOR: Tony Scott
CAST:
Will Smith
Gene Hackman
Regina King
Scott Caan

*Available on Video

Television Series

The Fresh Prince Of Bel Air
(NBC-TV 1990–1996)
CAST:
Will Smith
James Avery
Janet Hubert-Whitten
(later replaced by Daphne
Maxwell Reid)
Karyn Parsons
Tatyana M. Ali
Alfonso Ribeiro
Joseph Marcell
Ross Bagley
Jeff Townes (recurring role)

Discography

*As The Fresh Prince of the duo
"D.J. Jazzy Jeff & The Fresh
Prince":*

Rock the House *(Zomba/Jive/
RCA Records 1987)*
1. Girls Ain't Nothing But
   Trouble
2. Just One of Those Days
3. Rock the House
4. Taking It to the Top
5. The Magnificent Jazzy Jeff
6. Just Rockin'
7. Guys Ain't Nothing But
   Trouble (featuring Ice
   Cream Tee)

8. A Touch of Jazz
9. Don't Even Try It
10. Special Announcement

He's the D.J., I'm the Rapper
(Zomba/Jive/RCA Records 1988)
1. Nightmare on My Street
2. Here We Go Again
3. Brand New Funk
4. Time to Kill
5. Charlie Mack (1st Out of the Limo)
6. As We Go
7. Parents Just Don't Understand*
8. Pump Up the Bass
9. Let's Get Busy Baby
10. Live at Union Square (November 1986)
11. D.J. On the Wheels
12. My Buddy
13. Rhythm TraxHouse Party Style
14. He's the D.J., I'm the Rapper
15. Hip Hop Dancer's Theme
16. Jazzy's in the House
17. Human Video Game

And in This Corner *(Zomba/Jive/RCA Records 1989)*
1. Then She Bit Me
2. I Think I Can Beat Mike Tyson
3. Jazzy's Groove
4. Everything that Glitters (Ain't Always Gold)
5. You Got It (Donut)
6. The Girlie Had a Mustache
7. The Reverend
8. Who Stole My Car?
9. The Man of Your Dreams
10. Numero Uno
11. Too Damn Hype
12. Jeff Waz on the Beat Box

Homebase *(Zomba/Jive/RCA Records 1991)*
1. I'm All That
2. Summertime*
3. The Things That U Do
4. This Boy Is Smooth
5. Ring My Bell

6. A Dog Is a Dog
7. Caught in the Middle (Love & Life)
8. Trapped on the Dance Floor
9. Who Stole the D.J.
10. You Saw My Bliniker
11. Dumb Dancin'
12. Summertime (Reprise)

Code Red *(Zomba/Jive/RCA Records 1993)*
1. Somethin' Like Dis
2. I'm Looking for the One (To Be With Me)
3. Boom! Shake the Room
4. Can't Wait to Be With You (featuring Christopher Williams)

5. Twinkle Twinkle (I'm Not a Star)
6. Code Red
7. Shadow Dreams
8. Just Kickin' It
9. Ain't No Place Like Home
10. I Wanna Rock
11. Scream
12. Boom! Shake The Room (Street Remix)

Jazzy Jeff & the Fresh Prince Greatest Hits
(Zomba/Jive/RCA Records 1998)
1. Girls Ain't Nothing But Trouble
2. Men in Black*

3. Summertime*
4. Parents Just Don't Understand*
5. Boom! Shake the Room
6. Just Cruisin'
7. Ring My Bell
8. Brand New Funk
9. Lovely Daze
10. The Fresh Prince of Bel Air
11. Nightmare on My Street
12. A Touch of Jazz
13. I Think I Can Beat Mike Tyson
14. The Magnificent Jazzy Jeff
15. I'm Looking for the One (To Be With Me)
16. You Saw My Blinker
17. Summertime '98
18. Megamix

As Will Smith:

Big Willie Style *(Columbia Records 1997)*
1. Intro
2. Y'All Know
3. Gettin' Jiggy Wit It
4. Candy (featuring Larry Blackmon and Cameo)
5. Chasing Forever
6. Keith B. Real I (Interlude)
7. Don't Say Nothin'
8. Miami
9. Yes Yes Y'All (featuring Camp Lo)
10. I Loved You
11. Keith B. Real II (Interlude)
12. It's All Good
13. Just The Two Of Us
14. Keith B. Real III (Interlude)
15. Big Willie Style (featuring Left Eye)
16. Men In Black*

* *Grammy Award Winner*

Performing his song "Gettin' Jiggy Wit It" at the Grammy Awards, February 25, 1998.

The world that he had saved on the big screen in <u>Independence Day</u> was the same one on which he was now sitting firmly atop.